Lindy S. Adams

R Scott Lamascus

Decades of Destiny

A History of Churches of Christ
from 1900 - 2000

Lindy Adams & Scott LaMascus, Editors

HillCrest
PUBLISHING

Decades of Destiny: A History of Churches of Christ from 1900 - 2000

HillCrest
PUBLISHING

1648 Campus Court
Abilene, TX 79601
www.hillcrestpublishing.com

This book was designed and set into type by Nancy Love. The text faces are Warnock Pro, designed by Robert Slimbach in 2000 and Myriad Condensed, designed by Carol Twombly & Robert Slimbach in 1992. The display text is set in Engravers, designed by Robert Wiebking in 1899.

Cover photo: Union Avenue Church of Christ, Memphis, Tennessee

Acknowledgements
The photographs in this book are reproduced by permission of the following: Michael Casey; Center for Restoration Studies, Abilene Christian University; John Allen Chalk; Christian Chronicle archives; Doug Foster; Gospel Advocate Company; Gospel Services, Searcy, AR; Heritage Christian University (formerly International Bible College); Richard Hughes; Let's Start Talking, Department of Missions & Ministry, Abilene Christian University; Letters and Sermons of T. B. Larimore; Lipscomb University; Chad Longley, Special Collections Brown Library, Abilene Christian University; Elizabeth Mason; Lynn McMillon Collection; Ted Parks; Pepperdine University; Woodland Hills Church of Christ, Memphis, TN.

Printed in the United States of America

ISBN 0-89112-041-6

Library of Congress Card Number 2003116055

ACKNOWLEDGEMENTS

To Daddy, who taught me to love Restoration history, and to Ken, Elliott, and Elizabeth Corinne

-LSA

To The Christian Chronicle *staff and National Council, and to Parker and Hadley LaMascus*

-RSL

CONTENTS

LIST OF CONTRIBUTORS

Dr. Douglas A. Foster is professor of church history and Director of the Center for Restoration Studies at Abilene Christian University. He is co-author of *The Crux of the Matter: Crisis, Tradition, and the Future of Churches of Christ* and *Renewing God's People: A Concise History of Churches of Christ*. He serves as a deacon at the Minter Lane Church of Christ in Abilene.

Dr. Robert Hooper is author of *Crying in the Wilderness: A Biography of David Lipscomb* and is retired professor of church history from Lipscomb University. He is an elder at Woodmont Hills Church of Christ in Nashville, Tennessee.

Dr. Lynn A. McMillon is Distinguished Professor of Bible and Dean, College of Biblical Studies, at Oklahoma Christian University. He is an elder of the Memorial Road Church of Christ and author of *Restoration Roots.*

Dr. Michael W. Casey is the Carl P. Miller Chair of Communication at Pepperdine University. Casey is a member of the University Church of Christ in Malibu, California.

Dr. Thomas H. Olbricht is Distinguished Professor of Religion Emeritus at Pepperdine University. He lives in retirement in South Berwick, Maine, continuing to publish books and essays on Restoration History, Rhetorical Analysis of Scriptures, and Biblical Theology.

Dr. Steven S. Lemley is Associate Professor of Communication at Pepperdine University, Malibu, California. He is editor of *Power for Today*.

Dr. Richard T. Hughes is Distinguished Professor of Religion at Pepperdine University and Director of the Pepperdine Center for Faith and Learning. He is author of *Reviving the Ancient Faith: The Story of Churches of Christ in America* (Eerdmans, 1996).

Dr. R. Scott LaMascus is the Managing Editor of *The Christian Chronicle* and an Associate Professor of American Literature at Oklahoma Christian University. He is a member of the Memorial Road Church of Christ in Oklahoma City.

Dr. John Mark Hicks is Professor of Theology at Lipscomb University and Adult Education Minister for the Woodmont Hills Church of Christ in Nashville, Tennessee. He publishes materials at http://johnmarkhicks.faithsite.com.

FOREWORD

THIS book constitutes a brief but extremely informative history of Churches of Christ for the 20th century. As such, it will be especially useful in Bible classes and small study groups that want to explore the various factors that have contributed to defining Churches of Christ as the 21st century unfolds.

Each chapter also features an explanation of key terms, important quotations, links to websites, and discussion questions that can prompt serious reflection and lively discussion.

Those of us who participated in the creation of this book, along with the *Chronicle* staff, have high hopes for this volume. First, we offer it to the church in the hope that it will contribute to a greater historical awareness on the part of Churches of Christ.

But historical awareness surely cannot be an end in itself. Rather, we hope that our growing historical awareness will prompt individual Christians and congregations to recommit themselves to lives of meaningful discipleship, based not on the vagaries of history and culture, but based instead on the mandates of the Lord Jesus Christ. If this book bears fruit in that way, then we can hope for nothing more.

Dr. Richard T. Hughes

EDITORS' INTRODUCTION

IN 1999, the editorial round-table of *The Christian Chronicle* began discussing how to help readers, churches, and Christian families through the upheavals and shifts at the beginning of the 21st century.

How could we put into print significant materials that would help Christians keep their eyes on the unchanging gospel during times of rapid change? How could we help church members rediscover their roots in our fellowship and the beautiful verities of those roots — our deep beliefs in scriptural authority, congregational autonomy, the priesthood of all believers? How could we report honestly on the conflicts raging in many congregations without letting the mere fact of reporting and discussion fuel more fires? At this historic end of one century and beginning of another, how could we both remember the past and examine the present honestly, and in the process build the sense of community we love and cherish—the stuff of story for future generations?

We prayed. We went back to our mission to inform, inspire, and unite churches of Christ through journalistic excellence. We explored many options.

The result was *Restoration 21,* a series whose title tried to capture both forward- and backward-looking strategies for church health and vigor—a restoration movement for the new millennium. The series was grounded in a sense of optimism and becoming, of commitment to restoration for the present without losing sight of our immediate past.

As body and soul, we must acknowledge both history and eternity. It is not an easy task, but congregations and Christians across the land seem to be intently focused on the Cross and finding their way on a journey toward a biblical calling. We wanted to help them.

Thus, our series provided two parts: "Restoration Retrospective," which put 20th-century history into capsule form; and the issues-oriented articles that tried to identify key matters over which churches must study and pray. The historical material moved decade-by-decade through the century. The issues ranged from race relations to worship styles to women in the church. Both parts together comprised *Restoration 21.*

The resulting series also roughly paralleled a total redesign of *The Christian Chronicle* for the 21st century. This redesign was a real stretch for our small group, a few people who toil to make *The Christian Chronicle* appear in the household mail each month—for more than 100,000 Christian families across the nation and on the web for readers around the world. The process was comprehensive and required the combined efforts of many, including Bailey McBride, editor; Lynn McMillon, general manager; Glover Shipp, senior editor; Dale Jones and Jessica Olson, advertising managers; and Gwen Antwine, office manager. Many others played key roles in the brain trust and energy trust that made the unprecedented series possible, including Joy McMillon, a past managing editor and now leader of an important women's Bible study ministry, and, of course, our collaborators for this volume.

Our first thanks go to these people who made *Restoration 21* possible.

Chronicle readers, too, played a key role in the development of *Restoration 21.* Fully aware of the limits of only a few people writing a history of the entire 20th century, we were counseled to open the process to as many voices as possible. Readers responded eagerly. They sent letters to the editor. They e-mailed nominations for the events that— and people who— should be featured in each decade.

We posted this input in our online editions and have included the nominations as an appendix to this volume as testimony to the many men and women who led and served during these 100 years.

Toward the end of that year, as the 21st century loomed before us, Scott LaMascus introduced an installment of *Restoration 21* materials in the *Chronicle* by writing: *"When Ezra Pound longs in his* Cantos *for a day when the historians would leave 'blanks in their writings,' he was pointing out an important feature of history – that history and historians must be aware of how much they do not yet know. History dawns on us slowly, as our insights into the past grow. Time is an essential ingredient in the making of history because it enables us to know more about the subject at hand."* That sense of the incompleteness of history remains with us even as this book has developed. It is with great humility that we and our collaborators have tried to paint clear pictures of times that remain vivid in living memory.

Emotions of some of these events remain raw or heightened. Leaders of the 1940s remain alive, revered Fathers and Mothers of Israel. The most hotly contested bits of our 20th-century history continue to be the scene of struggle between factions or parties. The 1980s and 1990s remain too fresh to see clearly. We *still* know too little to fill in all the blanks.

We also must admit that some blanks could be filled—and should be—but were beyond our time and scope. For example, Lindy Adams repeatedly has worked to gather information on women who have shaped our congregations and our fellowship. Our histories must tell their stories with accuracy and appreciation, even as they describe an era often only referred to in our fellowship as a "brotherhood." Likewise, our history here suffers from the gap of color, the ways in which our history has been shaped by the color lines of the 20th-century church.

Histories of the century must take into account the many roles played by African American and Hispanic and Asian Christians in the United States. Another blank is the story of the church abroad, the thousands of congregations around the world whose stories have not been included here. History must tell these stories.

Readers of this volume will find some features of our original print series – short essays discussing each decade of the 20th century as well as even briefer descriptions of events and newsmaking persons for each decade. These materials were written by our collaborators—historians, scholars, and leaders. A table of contributors is provided for readers unfamiliar with these writers.

Other parts of this volume were great ideas that wouldn't fit into our print edition series in 2000: key terms and people, resource locators, bibliographies, and discussion questions. Bibliographic entries, not included in the newspaper version of the series, here follow the MLA style for simplicity. Submitted individually by the authors, these highly selective bibliographies have been combined by the editors for readers' convenience. They give a sense of the rich trove of history yet to be sorted out in a more systematic way.

A curriculum guide suggests how to use this book in Bible classes, book groups, and small group studies. Thom Lemmons and the ACU Press have helped us include these materials in the book, and we hope these details make the essays more useful as university students, small groups, elderships, and Bible classes take up the question of how to capture the unchanging in times of change.

In truth, much can be learned here from our most recent history. For example, it becomes clearer how the ideal of "brotherhood," our term for ourselves at mid-century, expressed a sense of fellowship, informality, and autonomy. The term also clearly reflects the sense in which women were "auxiliary" members, as Steven Lemley puts it in his essay here. How can we maintain integrity with scripture and face a new era in which *all* Christians are neither slave nor free, male nor female?

This is one of our most daunting challenges of the 21st century.

Another challenge issuing from recent history is in the area of racial and ethnic diversity. How can we speak to our diverse communities, cities, and towns—where diversity is as rich as it was at the turn of the 20th century when immigrants filled our cities? How can our elderships and ministry teams reflect the diversity of our faith communities today? It is another difficult but important challenge.

Or perhaps history is teaching us about the powerful personalities who found themselves in or projected themselves onto the most defining moments of American life in the 20th century. Regarding missions, Otis Gatewood comes to mind. Norvel Young is a clear example for domestic church growth. The personalities behind the service-oriented ministries of the Central church in Nashville defined our best response to the Great Depression. Carl Spain, Marshall Keeble, Fred Gray, A. M. Burton—and so many others—were key figures in helping us face the challenges of our times.

Be sure to study our list of nominations in the Appendices, because the book could easily have been expanded to include many of these Christians whose lives shaped the century. We need a new generation of leaders with their sterling qualities. These leaders also teach us to live lives of humility, for their lives have not been immune to the fires of suffering, sin, and error.

The lessons of history are myriad. They do not supercede scripture, of course, but the Old Testament reminds us of the importance of looking to those who have gone before us and remembering how easy it is to fail, like David, though we have a heart afire. How easy, like Samuel, to lose our children to save a kingdom. How easy, like Sarah, to give up hope before the Lord's promises come to pass. In the 19th century, many Christians held to the practice of teaching their young people the Bible, the lives of the early Christian martyrs, and the biographies of Christian leaders. Our generation could do worse.

Some editing matters require comment here. First, readers may be either distracted by or pleased to find a lower-case usage for the congregations when thought of as a body, that is, in the phrase *churches of Christ.* With this exception, we have adopted the Associated Press stylebook for our texts, since the essays originally were published in a newspaper. AP calls for upper-case usage, that is, *Churches of Christ.* Within the churches themselves, an upper-case usage has become more common, particularly in academic publishing. However, we have chosen to defer to the practice of retaining the lower-case "c," which seems to have represented a widespread commitment to non-denominational ideals. Allowing this signifier to appear here represents the churches' long-standing resistance to hierarchical organizations for intercongregational relationships.

This resistance alone, an historical and sociological fact in itself, justifies retention of the older habit in a book about our history of the 20th century, a time when the typographic practice was widespread if not universal. To capitalize the "c" makes those arguments invisible. Such an erasure does not build community, at the least, and, at the worst, might be haughty or ahistorical. Like every history, this book must be selective, but it is not our intention to commit acts of erasure here. Substantive discussion of this matter, however, should occur elsewhere.

Second, we have chosen to follow the original series published in *The Christian Chronicle* by refraining from the selection of a person or event to represent the history of the last two decades of the century. The 1980s and 1990s provide overview essays, only listing several persons and events of key importance. Although our vantage point from the time of editing this volume gives us a little more perspective, we still believe it is premature to select a single person or event as the most critical.

Richard T. Hughes and Douglas A. Foster have been generous collaborators and encouragers, first as we struggled with the series and, later, when we were uncertain whether or not to turn our Restoration 21 series into a book. Hughes advised us on numerous occasions, encouraged us, and generously agreed to write the Foreword to this volume. Likewise, Foster loaned us material, sent us encouraging notes, and listened to our complaints. Not least of his contributions is that he undertook to write an essay, "19ᵗʰ Century Origins," as a precursor to the 20ᵗʰ century overview that we already had undertaken.

Foster's essay was not part of the series published in *The Christian Chronicle*, but it could have been and would have added strength to our readers' understanding of the 20ᵗʰ century. We hope our book is a deserving sequel to Gary Holloway's and Foster's *Renewing God's People: A Concise History of Churches of Christ* (ACU Press, 2002), a detailed study of the nineteenth century and an overview of the twentieth.

Lindy S. Adams
Scott LaMascus
Oklahoma City
December 2003

Nineteenth Century Origins

UNITY AND DIVISION

"Whom God hath thus joined together, no man should dare to put asunder."
from **"THE DECLARATION AND ADDRESS"**

THE NECESSITY OF HISTORY   There scarcely is a family today that is not touched by the memory-robbing Alzheimers disease. Eventually those afflicted no longer remember who they are or even to whom they are related. Because they have lost their past, their present and future lack meaning. Everyone would agree Alzheimers is a horrible condition. Yet some Christians seem to suffer from self-induced amnesia! They know little of their history and don't think it matters. Failure of memory, whether produced by disease, injury, or neglect, has the same devastating results.

Having a sense of history–a "historical consciousness"–doesn't mean wanting to go back to the "good old days." Nor does it mean becoming a professional historian. It does mean knowing something about the people, ideas, and events that have shaped you. And just as important, it means always asking the historical questions: "Where did she get that idea?" "When and why has this issue come up before?" "How have past Christians dealt with this matter?"

We know to ask "What does the Bible say?" when faced with decisions about future directions and present problems. But we have seldom asked the historical questions because we didn't think they were relevant. In reality, developing a historical consciousness is one of the abilities God provided to help us mature in him.

Paul warned the Corinthians in 1 Corinthians 10:1-12 that, if they refused to learn from their history, they were in grave danger. The same is true today. If we ignore our history, if we think we can stand without it, we are in danger of serious failure.

This volume is about the people and events that shaped churches of Christ in the twentieth century. In this chapter, however, we examine our nineteenth-century roots as a movement to bring Christian unity by restoring a simple New Testament gospel.

CALVINISM: The teachings of John Calvin and his followers. They emphasized God's absolute sovereignty and humanity's sinfulness and corruption. Taught God had predestined who would be saved.

THE BACKGROUND OF THE STONE-CAMPBELL MOVEMENT

Most nineteenth-century churches were Calvinist, viewing humans as utterly sinful and incapable of responding to God. In contrast, Enlightenment ideals held human ability in high esteem. Common Sense philosophers like Thomas Reid emphasized the reliability of reason. Francis Bacon insisted that, by applying the scientific method, no knowledge was beyond human grasp. John Locke contended that Christianity was reasonable and that only things clearly taught in the New Testament should be made terms of communion.

ENLIGHTENMENT: An eighteenth-century intellectual movement that emphasized the ability of human reason to discover truth for itself without the need for religious, political, or other authorities.

Unlike European philosophers, Americans believed that everyone, not just a few elites, shared the same reasoning ability. Able to understand the Bible free from the domination of a state church and clergy, many set out to reform the church in this God-prepared land.

Among these reformers was Methodist minister James O'Kelly. In 1793, he and others in North Carolina and Virginia judged Methodist church government under authoritative bishops unscriptural and formed the Republican Methodist Church. The next year, however, they dropped that name and called themselves simply Christians.

In New England, Elias Smith and Abner Jones rejected the Calvinism of their Baptist heritage and began establishing Christian churches in the early 1800s. A few years later in Tennessee, a group of Presbyterians, led by Finis Ewing, Samuel King, and Samuel McAdow, also rejected Calvinism and formed the Cumberland Presbyterian Church. It would be three other Presbyterians who would lead in forming the movement that produced the Churches of Christ.

THE DEVELOPMENT OF THE STONE AND CAMPBELL MOVEMENTS BARTON W. STONE (1772-1844) Barton Warren Stone was born in Port Tobacco, Maryland on December 24, 1772. Though baptized an Anglican at birth, religion was not a major part of Stone's early life. At age 18, he traveled to North Carolina to study law under Presbyterian minister David Caldwell. Caldwell, a "New Light," favored revivals and rejected strict adherence to the Westminster Confession, the Presbyterian creed.

After arriving at Caldwell's Academy, Stone was convicted of his sinful state by the preaching of James McGready. Failing to have a conversion experience as taught by the Presbyterians, he agonized for weeks. Finally, under the preaching of another Presbyterian revivalist, William Hodge, he was convinced of God's love and of his own salvation, and committed himself to the ministry.

In 1796, Stone became licensed to preach. He traveled first in North Carolina and middle Tennessee, then moved to Bourbon County, Kentucky to preach for the Cane Ridge and Concord Churches near Paris. In 1798, these churches called him to be their regular minister, a call that led Stone to a crisis, for he had doubts about parts of the Westminster Confession, especially its Calvinism and doctrine of the Trinity.

An obelisk at the Disciples of Christ Historical Society, Nashville, Tennessee, bears the images of Alexander Campbell and Barton W. Stone

Fortunately, the Transylvania Presbytery consisted of ministers who, like Stone, had been influenced by New Light ideas. When asked if he accepted the Westminster Confession, he replied in typical New Light fashion, "I do, as far as I see it consistent with the word of God," and was ordained.

In the Spring of 1801, Stone journeyed to Logan County, Kentucky to witness the dramatic conversions he had heard about under the preaching of James McGready. The services were Presbyterian sacramental meetings—the annual taking of the Lord's Supper. Preachers prepared the saved for the solemn occasion and warned sinners of their fate. Stone was astonished at what he saw—people were struck down, sometimes for hours, then rose to embrace Christ and live changed lives.

After his return home, he called a sacramental meeting at Cane Ridge for early August. Between twelve and twenty thousand people came, along with forty Presbyterian, Methodist, and Baptist preachers who preached Christ without denominational distinction. The ecstatic exercises Stone had seen in Logan County were multiplied at Cane Ridge. He saw many converted and was thrilled at the unity the meeting promoted.

The Synod of Kentucky, however, was not happy about Cane Ridge. They moved against Stone's colleague, Richard McNemar, in September 1803. As a result, McNemar, Stone, and three other ministers withdrew and formed their own Springfield Presbytery. In June 1804, however, they "killed" it with *The Last Will and Testament of the Springfield Presbytery*, the first foundational document of the movement. The opening clause reads, "We will that this body die, be dissolved, and sink into union with the body of Christ at large." At the suggestion of Rice Haggard, formerly of the O'Kelly movement, they too began simply calling themselves Christians.

Though eventually deserted by most of his original colleagues, Stone continued to preach. Soon there were churches affiliated with his movement from Alabama and Missouri to Indiana and Illinois.

THOMAS (1763-1854) AND ALEXANDER CAMPBELL (1788-1866)

Thomas Campbell and his son Alexander were Presbyterians from Northern Ireland, members of a division of the Church of Scotland called the Associate Synod. Thomas became a leader in the Synod and worked to break down barriers separating the groups. His failing to bring unity, along with overwork in preaching and teaching, led to serious health problems, and his doctor prescribed a long sea voyage. Though reluctant, Campbell departed for America in April 1807, a move already made by thousands of Irish people before him.

When he arrived in Philadelphia, the American leaders of his church were meeting. He presented his credentials, was cordially received and assigned to preach in western Pennsylvania. His disgust for the divisions in the church was still strong. For example, when Presbyterians not part of his group came to his service, he offered the Communion to everyone, which led to a trial before the Presbytery and then the Synod in Philadelphia. By the Spring of 1809, Campbell had completely severed his ties with the Associate Synod–he was a man without a church. Yet many to whom he had ministered in western Pennsylvania still supported him in his efforts toward Christian unity.

In August 1809, Campbell and several friends organized the Christian Association of Washington, Pennsylvania to promote "evangelical" Christianity based on the Bible alone. Campbell's explanation of the aims and beliefs of the Association, titled *The Declaration and Address*, became the movement's second foundational document. Campbell clearly saw this effort as an attempt to bring about Christian unity. Two of the most quoted parts of the lengthy pamphlet assert that "The Church of Christ upon earth is essentially, intentionally, and constitutionally one," and "division among Christians is a horrid evil, [filled] with many evils."

In the meantime, Campbell's family, led by 21-year-old Alexander, finally arrived in New York on September 27 (after an attempt a year earlier had ended in shipwreck). Alexander too had renounced the exclusive sectarianism of the Associate Synod.

When he and his father reunited and compared experiences, it was clear they were of the same mind.

After an unsuccessful attempt to unite with the Presbyterian Church in the United States, the Christian Association was organized as an independent congregation in May 1811, named after Brush Run Creek. The eloquent Alexander Campbell soon became the chief spokesperson for the movement.

Alexander's marriage and the birth of his first child forced a decision regarding infant baptism. After careful study, he concluded that it was not warranted by scripture and that he needed to conform to New Testament baptism. On June 12, 1812, Alexander, his wife Margaret, his parents, his sister Dorothea, and two other members of the Brush Run Church were immersed by Baptist minister Matthias Luce following their simple professions of faith. Others followed and, although some could not accept the practice, soon Brush Run was a congregation of immersed believers.

"I will not say there are no faults in brother Campbell; but that there are fewer, perhaps, in him, than any man I know on earth; and over these few my love would throw a veil, and hide them from view forever. ... The Lord reward him!"

- BARTON W. STONE,
Autobiography, 1843

The Campbells believed they should work within existing Christianity, so in 1813 the Brush Run Church became part of the Redstone Baptist Association. For over fifteen years, the churches of the Campbell movement were known as "reforming" or "Reformed Baptists." In the late 1820s, tensions rose over understandings of baptism, adherence to the Philadelphia Confession of Faith, and Calvinist doctrine. Congregations sympathetic to the Campbells' ideas were expelled from Baptist Associations, becoming known simply as disciples of Christ.

THE UNION The Stone and Campbell movements differed in important ways. Some were "surface" issues like the name. Though both used names intended to avoid separating themselves from other believers, the Stone churches preferred "Christian" and the Campbell churches "disciples." At one point, Stone accused Campbell of avoiding the name Christian for fear it would associate his movement with undesirables.

But there were more serious matters, like the practice of open membership. The early Stone movement welcomed all who wanted to join themselves to the reform— even the unimmersed. Though Campbell believed there were true Christians who had not been immersed (see the "Lunenburg Letter" articles in the 1837 *Millennial Harbinger*), he believed that scriptural baptism depicted the immersion of believers. The churches of his reformation, therefore, insisted on it.

The differences did not stop there: they included conflicting understandings of the Trinity, the atonement, the work of the Holy Spirit, human nature, evangelistic methods, and the second coming of Christ. These were not minor disagreements! The movements were as diverse as today's churches of Christ and United Pentecostal Church.

Yet they shared certain things that superceded the differences, especially their dogged commitment to three beliefs: Jesus Christ is the Messiah; the Bible is the supreme and final authority in all religious matters; and since Christ's church is one, Christians ought to act like it—despite differences on various matters.

As the two movements spread, they had increasing contact in places like Kentucky, Indiana, and Ohio. They found kindred spirits in each other and, in the late 1820s, many began to ask why they could not be one. Alexander Campbell was uneasy

OPEN MEMBERSHIP: The practice of allowing unimmersed persons to become members of a congregation. Churches in the Stone movement practiced "open membership" early. It later became a matter of division in the movement.

about the supposed non–orthodox doctrines of the Stone churches. Yet, in several places, local congregations did unite.

During the week of Christmas 1831, preachers, elders, and members from the two movements met first at Georgetown, Kentucky and then at the Hill Street Christian church in Lexington to discuss what they might do. On Saturday, December 31, John Smith from the Reformers and Barton Stone from the Christians spoke. Smith urged his listeners, "Let us no longer be New Lights or Old Lights, Campbellites or Stoneites, or any other kind of lights, but let us come to the only book that can give us all the light we need."

Those present agreed to become one, sealing the union by sharing the Lord's Supper on Sunday, January 1, 1832. John Rodgers from the Stone movement and John Smith from the Campbell movement traveled together over the next three years telling what had happened at Lexington and helping consolidate the union in other places.

The union was not easy. Not all congregations participated. Yet leaders and members of both movements were committed to unity. Over the next decade in communities across the nation, churches of the two groups came together to form a new united movement.

The best estimate of the number of members in the united movement in 1832 is 22,000. By 1860, the movement had exploded to 195,000 members in over 2,100 churches. At least fifteen journals were published during the era, Alexander Campbell's *Millennial Harbinger* being the most significant. Others included Stone's *Christian Messenger* (1826-1845) and Walter Scott's *Evangelist* (1832-1842). Two papers would become especially influential after the Civil War–the *Gospel Advocate* (1855) and the *American Christian Review* (1856). Alexander Campbell and others published debates and doctrinal studies like *The Christian System* as well.

The establishment of colleges also reflected the movement's growth. Three of the earliest were Bacon College in Georgetown, Kentucky (1836), Bethany College in

Bethany, Virginia (1841), and Franklin College near Nashville, Tennessee (1845). Members of the movement established scores of academies and institutions of higher education before 1860, including the forerunners of Butler and Drake Universities.

These structures helped identify and define who we were. By the time Joseph Belcher's handbook of American denominations was published in 1857, we were listed as one of the ten largest religious bodies in the country.

THE DIVISION   Yet seeds of division were already being sown. The thrilling union of the Stone and Campbell churches in the 1830s would be marred by division at the end of the century. There had always been considerable diversity of thought in the churches, but now certain matters began to prove especially contentious.

One was the American Christian Missionary Society (ACMS), founded in Cincinnati in 1849. Some saw the organization as an expedient way of fulfilling Christ's command to teach the gospel to the whole world. Others, however, opposed it as a human institution, unauthorized by scripture. These positions reflected different beliefs over whether or not the silence of scripture prohibited or freed.

Yet even some of the missionary society's strongest critics did not see it as an issue over which to divide. Tolbert Fanning, founder of the *Gospel Advocate* and opponent of the society, spoke at its annual meeting in 1859, declaring "we are one people." It took a national disaster to change his mind.

With the outbreak of the Civil War, southerners could not attend ACMS meetings in Cincinnati. Pressured to show loyalty to the Union, the ACMS passed resolutions in 1861 and 1863 condemning the southern rebellion and asking God's blessing on the Union forces. When Fanning and others, who had desperately tried to keep the churches out of the bitter North-South conflict, heard of the resolution, they felt deeply betrayed. Fanning wrote in 1861, "How can the servants of the Lord of this section ever [shake] hands with the men who now seek their life's blood?" The Civil War played a powerful part in the eventual division.

A depiction of a baptism in a stained-glass window at the Disciples of Christ Historical Society, Nashville, Tennessee

After the war, the number of organizations grew to include the Christian Woman's Board of Missions (1874), the Foreign Christian Missionary Society (1875), and the National Benevolent Association (1887). Southern churches, represented by the *Gospel Advocate* and its new editor David Lipscomb (1831-1917), largely opposed them. Yet the opposition was not merely sectional–some in the north, including Benjamin Franklin (1812-1878) and Daniel Sommer (1850-1940), attacked these "innovations" through the pages of the *American Christian Review*.

The issue that became the most explosive—instrumental music in worship—also related to events of the Civil War. As early as October 1851, Alexander Campbell stated that "to all spiritually-minded Christians such aids would be as a cow bell in a concert." Only a few churches were using instruments at the time of the Civil War, the most famous at Midway, Kentucky, where L. L. Pinkerton introduced a melodeon to compensate for the group's awful singing.

After the Civil War, the northern economy prospered, but the south's was devastated. Northern churches erected new buildings, sometimes including expensive organs. Southerners resented their northern sisters and brothers spending huge sums on buildings and organs while they barely existed, adding a powerful emotional element to the opposition to instrumental music.

Many rural Christians in both north and south viewed instrumental music as an accommodation to worldly desires for entertainment, the opposite of simple worship from the heart. Along with the argument that it was not authorized in scripture and its "in your face" visibility, the sectional, economic, and sociological factors combined to make instrumental music the most volatile issue in the division. For many in churches of Christ, "the instrument" became a symbol for all the issues— the single visible criteria for whether a church was loyal or apostate.

By 1906, the U.S. Religious Census would list churches of Christ separately from the Disciples. The division between the churches of Christ and the Christian Churches (or Disciples) in the late 19th and early 20th centuries was a division between theological conservatives. The combatants all argued from the authority of scripture. Yet the beginning of a second division could already be seen, a division that would pit conservatives against liberals and result in the formation in 1968 of the Christian Church (Disciples of Christ) and a separate group of "independent" Christian Churches and churches of Christ.

CONCLUSION   The Stone-Campbell Movement from which churches of Christ grew began as an effort to bring unity among Christians by focusing on basic Christian faith as found in the New Testament. It produced two documents that still call believers to the unity Christ prayed for in the garden. Yet the movement suffered two major divisions, with other divisions occurring within each of the three "streams."

The rest of this volume is the story of one of those streams–the churches of Christ. Yet we cannot end this chapter without mentioning some encouraging events of the twentieth century. In 1984 the Restoration Forums began, bringing together

A page from the religious census of 1916, which first indicated a division between the Disciples of Christ and the Churches of Christ

sisters and brothers from churches of Christ and "independent" Christian Churches for dialogue, fellowship, and worship. These meetings promote understanding and cooperation between the groups. The Forums meet every Fall and are open to all. Many presentations from the meetings have been published, and reports appear regularly in *One Body* magazine.

In 1999, the Stone-Campbell Dialogue began, bringing together six members from each of the three streams for intense discussion about what we share and how we differ. The purpose statement is "To develop relationship and trust within the three streams of the Stone-Campbell movement through worship and through charitable and frank dialogue 'that the world may believe.'" All of these presentations are available at the web site http://www.disciples.org/ccu/stonecampbell.htm.

May we all faithfully commit to this rich heritage of unity and biblical Christianity as we enter the twenty-first century and as we write new chapters in our history.

- By Douglas A. Foster

Nineteenth Century Origins

DISCUSSION QUESTIONS

1. Explain Paul's point in I Corinthians 10:1-12. Why does he give the church a history lesson in the middle of discussing all their problems?
2. What do you see as the main religious and intellectual influences on the early Stone-Campbell Movement?
3. List and discuss as many similarities between the Stone and Campbell movements as you can. Then list as many differences as you can.
4. How did the union between the Stone and Campbell churches begin and progress?
5. How many factors were involved in the division between the churches of Christ and the Christian Churches/Disciples? What would you say was the single most significant difference?

CHALLENGE QUESTIONS:

1. What do you see as possible negative results of a church's lack of historical consciousness?
2. Why is it *not* surprising that the Stone-Campbell Movement arose when and where it did?
3. How would you describe the two founding documents of the Stone-Campbell Movement? In what ways might these documents be important for churches of Christ today?
4. Based on the differences between the Stone and Campbell Movements, how do you think they were able to unite? Would such a union be possible today?
5. Why did the issue of instrumental music in worship become such a significant matter in the movement? Do you believe it should have become as divisive as it did? Why or why not?

The faculty of the Nashville Bible School pictured during the decade of 1900-1910. David Lipscomb is on the back row, second from left.

1900-1910

A FELLOWSHIP DIVIDES

"Brother Lipscomb has stood, like a balance wheel, endeavoring to adhere always to the rational mean."
-JAMES A. ALLEN, *1909*

THE first decade of the 20th century was a time of celebration in the larger Stone-Campbell Movement. During the same decade of the previous century, both Stone and the Campbells had given leadership to restoration movements. Literally thousands of people on the frontier had accepted the pleas of the three men. Both movements had called for unity in the Christian community.

One hundred years later, unity remained the goal of various groups within the American Restoration Movement, but there were differences as to how the goal might be attained. In many ways, these differences define the first decade of the 20th century.

The defining characteristics of churches of Christ were certainly present in 1900 —opposition to the instrument in worship and opposition to missionary societies. However, the underlying cause of impending division was much more profound. To place the events in a larger context, the

STONE-CAMPBELL MOVEMENT: A religious movement of the early 19th century that called for all people to discard their sectarian views and unite on the Bible as the only basis for Christian unity.

Event of the Decade:
A Fellowship Divides

"Our position has been a peculiar one. We have been identified with a people that started out to return to unsectarian Bible Christianity. They have divided into two parties, each turning in different directions. We have stood between them."

-DAVID LIPSCOMB, 1907

The response from David Lipscomb to the questions of S. N. D. North, the director of the religious census, did not appear until 1907 in the pages of the *Gospel Advocate*. North had wanted to know if his perceptions were correct: are there at least two divisions within the Disciples of Christ? Lipscomb, sadly and reluctantly, responded in the affirmative. Among other things, Lipscomb stated: "There is a distinct people taking the word of God as their only sufficient rule of faith, calling their churches 'churches of Christ' or 'churches of God,' distinct and separate in name, work or rule of faith, from all other bodies or peoples." He then added: "They are purely congregational and independent in their polity and work...."

Lipscomb concluded his response to North: "Their aim is to unite all professed Christians in the sole purpose of promoting simple, evangelical Christianity as God revealed in the Scriptures...."

The division had been underway for many years, possibly since the formation of the American Christian Missionary Society in 1849. Alfred T. DeGroot, a Disciples' historian, believed the division occurred long before 1906. He recognized what Lipscomb also knew—events of the 1880s and the 1890s caused the division; the census only made it official. Daniel Sommer, editor of the *American Christian Review*, announced in 1889 that the division existed, prompting him to exclaim "Hallelujah!"

North even came to Nashville to instruct J. W. Shepherd, an *Advocate* employee, as to how the census should be taken. Shepherd discovered 159,658 members, a far cry from the nearly one million among Disciples of Christ.

From across the larger Disciples brotherhood, voices of surprise surfaced. Some within churches of Christ asked, "Who gave Lipscomb the right to speak for all of us?" James H. Garrison of the *Christian-Evangelist* even doubted that such a division was taking place. Despite the doubters, 1906 remains the official year when churches of Christ became a separate religious body in the United States.

What began in unity became division.

Stone-Campbell Movement was not the only religious movement in the process of splintering.

With the arrival of German liberal theology and its companion movement, Darwinism, American religion was on a collision course. The clash came early in the 20th century. The conservative outcome of the conflict became known as fundamentalism. Although churches of Christ did not participate in the larger movement, what happened in 1906 suggests a parallel course with the fundamentalists.

"DECLARATION AND ADDRESS:" A document written in 1909 by Thomas Campbell that defined his understanding as to how Christian unity might be attained.

Consequently, the years 1899-1909 define the separation within the American Restoration Movement. In 1899, led by David Lipscomb, conservative Disciples refused to participate in a celebration of the 50th anniversary of the founding of the American Christian Missionary Society. In 1909, the Disciples celebrated the 1804 writing of the *Declaration and Address.*

Although editors among churches of Christ noticed those events, it was primarily to emphasize the conflicts present among the participants. The editors of the *Christian-Evangelist* championed speakers who were considered liberal by the editors of the *Christian Standard.* The person most under attack was Herbert Willett of the Disciples House at the University of Chicago. John W. McGarvey, president and longtime teacher at College of the Bible in Lexington, Kentucky, was a relentless critic of Willett.

Just as fundamentalism defined conservative evangelicals, so the issues of the century's first decade defined conservative Disciples, especially churches of Christ. In addition to the issues of music, missionary

DISCIPLES OF CHRIST: A term Alexander Campbell favored to identify those persons who accept the tenets of the Stone-Campbell Movement. Stone preferred the term Christian.

Early home of David Lipscomb, now on the university campus

Decades of Destiny

THE "BROTHERHOOD": A term for describing what many now call our "fellowship" or our "tradition." As seen in the 1950s, the brotherhood was composed of people who were members of the churches of Christ and may have often especially been used to identify the mainline grouping of preachers, opinion leaders, and leaders of extra-church organizations related to the churches of Christ. Sisters were auxiliary members of the brotherhood.

societies, and liberal theology, the open espousal of women in public worship may have been the straw that tipped the scales toward division in David Lipscomb's mind.

Internally, the founding of schools also helped define a separate religious movement. In 1891, James A. Harding and David Lipscomb began the Nashville Bible School. In the same year that churches of Christ first were listed separately in the religious census, Abilene Christian College began as Childers Classical Institute (1906). These schools would teach and train the next generation of preachers and leaders within churches of Christ.

A 1909 photo at Childers Classical Institute, forerunner of Abilene Christian University, Abilene, Texas

Person of the Decade:
David Lipscomb

David Lipscomb (1831-1917) had lived beyond the lifetime of his peers. Yet, his influence was no less than it had been in his heyday as editor of the *Gospel Advocate*. Lipscomb was the person who penned the article to the director of the religious census indicating the presence of two groups within the Stone-Campbell Movement. The reason he could write the article and be readily accepted by his brethren was his leadership throughout the 34 years of his editorship of the paper. The defining characteristic of his theology and his editorship was moderation. He did not share the more radical views of Austin McGary, who had launched the *Firm Foundation* in 1884, or Daniel Sommer, publisher of the *American Christian Review*. Nor did he share the more progressive views of the *Christian-Evangelist* or even the *Christian Standard*. However, he knew what he believed. His editorials and especially his questions and answers in the *Advocate* helped to define the moderate position among conservatives. By 1900, his positions were clear on the major issues—music, missionary societies, women's role in worship, and higher criticism.

Lipscomb early came under the influence of Tolbert Fanning at Franklin College near Nashville, Tennessee. As he matured as an adult, he read deeply in the writings of Alexander Campbell. Therefore, when the *Gospel Advocate* faced difficult times in 1866, he stepped forward to edit and publish the paper. Not really desiring to become a leader among Disciples of Christ, he became the spokesman for southern moderate conservatives. It was only natural that he would speak for the broad middle of churches of Christ by 1906.

Opposition to the missionary societies certainly dominated the thinking of conservative Disciples in the nineteenth century. Non-missionary society churches did not begin supporting foreign missions until 1889, when Nashville churches supported Azariah Paul in his native Armenia. In 1891, J. M. McCaleb became the first person sent exclusively overseas, to Japan, by those who would become churches of Christ. The only major foreign mission until the first decade of the twentieth century, the Japanese mission helped to define churches of Christ in the early 20th century.

Although the instrument in worship had been a major issue since the 1850s, it was not openly debated until early in the 20th century. In 1903, Joe S. Warlick met J. Carroll Stark (instrument) in a discussion at Henderson, Tennessee. In 1908, J. B. Briney (instrument) met W. W. Otey in Louisville, Kentucky in debate over the instrument, another defining moment in churches of Christ.

The census of 1906 listed churches of Christ as having 159,658 members in 2,649 congregations. Although these numbers were not large, it was a beginning that would see substantial growth throughout the century.

- By Robert Hooper

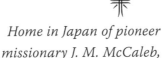

*Home in Japan of pioneer
missionary J. M. McCaleb,
now a historic site*

Home of David and Margaret Lipscomb on the university campus

1900-1910
A Fellowship Divides

DISCUSSION QUESTIONS

1. What made the conservative Disciples (Churches of Christ) a "distinct people?"
2. On what basis have churches of Christ called for unity?
3. Is it possible to be a "distinct people" in the 21st century? Explain your answer.

CHALLENGE QUESTIONS

1. What are the defining characteristics of churches of Christ in the 21st century? How do these characteristics relate to the views of Barton W. Stone and Alexander Campbell's call for Christian unity?
2. In what ways do churches of Christ remain a restoration movement?
3. Do the issues that led to division in 1906 remain issues today?
4. How can David Lipscomb be described as a moderate? Compare him with the ideas of Austin McGary and Daniel Sommer.

Class of 1918 with a banner from the days of Cordell Christian College

1910-1920

THE END OF PACIFISM

THE second decade of the century reflected both the effects of the earlier 1906 separation and the approaching "war to end all wars." Churches of Christ found themselves diminished in members, social prominence, and finances—first from the division and later from a pacifistic stance toward the war.

Churches of Christ struggled, in this decade of 1910-1920, both to reestablish themselves and to create a clear identity. These would not come easily. Underlying the thought of this period in America was the dichotomy between belief that the kingdom was being realized here and now versus belief in a kingdom of the future. Richard T. Hughes, in his *Reviving the Ancient Faith*, calls "apocalyptic" the view that God's final rule is here and now and thus one's loyalty was to God and not human governments.

"Instead of things getting better, the Spirit of God points to worse things ahead as the coming of the Lord draws near.... This dispensation, as those preceding, will end in a failure, fearful in proportion to the high privileges that were offered. As in the days of Noah, as in the days of Lot, the few will be delivered— those who are to be caught up to meet the Lord in the air."

-R. H. BOLL, *Truth and Grace,* 1917

45

The decade opened with a debate between James A. Harding and L. S. White, preacher for the Pearl and Bryan congregation in Dallas, on the subject of mutual edification versus located paid preachers. This debate reflected the shift that was occurring in the thinking of the church from itinerant preachers to paid located preachers. White himself might well be seen as a key role model for located paid preachers. A congenial and pleasant man, he was evangelistic, a church builder, and a debater. The largely rural and frontier church was now transitioning to a more established church with growing urban roots.

Pacifism was also a major underlying current of the period. Pacifism was linked to the belief that the church had been restored and thus allegiance was to be toward the kingdom rather than civil governments. Though the previous generation was mostly pacifistic, their children were not. David Lipscomb, who died in 1917, was the leading defender of pacifism.

Times, however, were changing. While J. N. Armstrong stepped down and Cordell Christian College in Cordell, Oklahoma closed in 1919 rather than change their pacifistic stand, Abilene Christian College established the Student's Army Training Corps in 1918 and saw its enrollment increase.

The mood of the times was greatly affected by The Great War of 1914–1918, and the U.S.'s entry into that war in 1917. The specter of war enhanced the prophetic and millennial teachings of Robert H. Boll (1875-1956). Boll opposed the prevalent view that society was becoming better and ever more progressive and that the war would make the world safe for democracy. Boll became the editor of the front-page column "Word and Work" in the *Gospel Advocate* in 1909. Very much in the thinking of the day, Boll began to consider the role of prophecy. As time passed, Boll argued that the church is not the completed and perfect kingdom of God. He stated that only when Christ returns to the earth would such a rule exist. Underlying Boll's views was his belief in God's grace and effort toward man. By the time he was pressured into resigning his column at the end of 1915, his premillennial views had been spread to a major segment of the church. Even men like James A. Harding shared the

Event of the Decade:
The Closing of Cordell Christian College Signals End of Pacifism

The closing of Cordell Christian College in Cordell, Oklahoma is the event of the decade because it reflects both the changing brotherhood and the end of pacifism as part of the change. Oklahoma became a state in 1907; Cordell Christian College opened in 1908. The board hired J. N. Armstrong, who had previously served with Nashville Bible School, to become president in 1909. Armstrong followed Lipscomb's views on civil government and declined to serve in the military.

Unfortunately, Armstrong encouraged noncombatant duty for Cordell students at a time when fervor for the war of 1914-1918 was growing. His views and those of his board and faculty did not go unnoticed. Even though a few students had enlisted in the army, the local Council of Defense in Cordell, in July 1918, required that the school reorganize to "conform to all military policies" to carry on the war effort. The Council of Defense further required the resignation of Armstrong and any faculty and board members who held these views. Refusing, Cordell Christian College closed in 1918, moving to Harper, Kansas in the fall of 1919.

Furthermore, Armstrong did not join other college presidents in condemning the premillennial teachings of Robert Boll in the *Gospel Advocate* that offered a prophetic and millennial escape from the war. Though pacifism in churches of Christ did not end entirely with World War I, Cordell's closing and the war signaled the shift of a majority of churches away from pacifism.

premillennial outlook.

Through this whole period, the nationwide preaching of T. B. Larimore may well have been the stabilizing factor. An indefatigable speaker, talking in more places that one can count, Larimore focused on gospel preaching. David Lipscomb once wrote in the *Gospel Advocate* that "Brother Larimore comes nearer reproducing the teaching of the Bible in his preaching than any man I know." Widely sought after, not only for his speaking ability, his clear and understandable teaching was needed in this turbulent decade. — Consultants: Douglas Foster and Mike Casey

- By Lynn A. McMillon

Early campus view, Cordell Christian College, Cordell, Oklahoma

Person of the Decade:
T. B. Larimore's Positive Preaching
Influence and his 'Boys'

A strong case might be made to select Robert Boll, James A. Harding, J. N. Armstrong, or others as the person of this decade. T. B. Larimore (1843-1929) is highlighted mainly because of his positive preaching influence across the nation and because of the lasting nature of his work through his "boys" for more than two generations. Though he was one of the great minds of the period, he did not become enmeshed in the controversies of the day.

In 1871, Larimore and his wife began the Mars Hill College near Florence, Alabama, where he worked until overwhelming demands for his preaching moved him to close the school in 1887. His "boys" were encouraged to return to their own homes and to the backwoods of the South to preach. Larimore literally received piles of mail pleading for him to hold protracted meetings in—or even relocate to—various places. Those calls he could not refuse, and he preached extensively throughout Alabama, Georgia, Florida, Mississippi, Louisiana, Tennessee, Kentucky, and Texas.

In 1891, he refused the presidency of Nashville Bible School because of his commitment to evangelism. His last 20 years found him spending increasingly greater amounts of time in California.

His contemporaries portray him as one of the purest, kindest Christian men one could ever meet. His preaching reflected an almost inexhaustible source of Bible knowledge. He represents the best.

T. B. Larimore — "a baptizing and a sprinkling"

1910-1920
The End of Pacifism

DISCUSSION QUESTIONS

1. What were the effects of the WWI era on your congregation (if it had been established by that time)? On your family — parents, grandparents, great-grandparents?

2. What are the views of Christian participation in the military today? How does Scripture shape our thinking on Pacifism or militarism?

3. Reflect on the stabilizing influence of any individual in your congregation or in the larger circle of Christianity. What characteristics do these modern-day T. B. Larimores share?

SARAH ANDREWS (1893-1961) was the pioneering missionary who served from 1916 to 1961 in Japan - beginning a public nursery, establishing women's societies, and sharing the gospel. Her work produced eight congregations.

CHALLENGE QUESTIONS

1. What does Richard Hughes mean by the term "apocalyptic"? How did this view influence church members' beliefs about human governments? military service?

2. Who was the leading defender of pacifism during this time? What is he most famous for today?

3. How did the pacifism of J. N. Armstrong and David Lipscomb affect the lives of the generation born at the turn of the century (your grandparents or great-grandparents)? Are there any remnants of this belief surviving in the church today?

4. What did Robert H. Boll, a proponent of the "apocalyptic" view, believe about human progress? About the reign of Christ in the end times?

5. How did the carnage of World War I (1914-18), in light of its aim to be the "war to end all wars," fuel the apocalyptic strain evident in the church in this century? How did events such as the sinking of the Titanic fuel this strain?

The imposing building of the Union Avenue Church of Christ, Memphis, Tennessee, which opened in 1925, typified the increase in the number and quality of church edifices. Today the building houses the Midtown congregation.

1920-1930

FUNDAMENTALIST CONTROVERSY

"I have never been so egotistical to say that my brethren with whom I commune ... are the only Christians on this earth. I never said that in my life. I do make the claim that we are Christians only."
-N. B. HARDEMAN, Hardeman Tabernacle Sermons *v.3, p.12*

THE decade of the 1920s was a period of numeric and economic growth for the churches of Christ. According to the U.S. Census Bureau, the movement swelled from 317,937 members in 1916 to 433,714 members in 1926. From 1916 to 1926, 656 new churches were established, 785 new buildings constructed, and 995 new Sunday schools were created with an increase of 106,000 students. The indebtedness of the churches of Christ for church buildings increased from $5,644,096 in 1916 to $16,402,158 in 1926. Large, expensive buildings were constructed in urban areas. For example, the Union Avenue congregation in Memphis built a large structure for $125,000 in 1925, using modern advertising and promotional schemes to attract members. James A. Allen, editor of the *Gospel Advocate*, argued that the building was extravagant and "a satire on the spirit and genus of Christianity."

A. M. BURTON (1879-1966), founder and president of Life and Casualty insurance company, helped establish Central Church of Christ (Nashville, Tennessee); sponsored Marshall Keeble's evangelistic efforts; chairman of the Board of Trustees, David Lipscomb College.

Event of the Decade:
The Fundamentalist-Modernist Controversy at Abilene Christian College

During the 1920s, the Fundamentalist-Modernist controversies dominated American religion. While remaining aloof from the denominations, the churches of Christ did not escape these issues. Abilene Christian College, under Jesse Sewell's leadership, offered unaccredited graduate work in Bible. As a means to gain accreditation for the program, William Webb Freeman, a professor of Bible, took a leave of absence to pursue a Ph.D. in New Testament at Yale University. In 1922, Freeman wrote an article in the *Firm Foundation* claiming that the Bible was infallible in the area of religion, but not in the area of science. Freeman was fired from ACC by Sewell, and a nine-month-long controversy over theories of inspiration and evolution ensued. Suspicious of his Yale education, G. H. P. Showalter and G. C. Brewer accused Freeman of being a modernist. Freeman moved to Commerce, Texas, where he became a successful professor at East Texas State University and an elder at the local congregation. The controversy eventually ended this effort at graduate education in 1924 with Jesse Sewell leaving ACC. Two of Freeman's and Sewell's students, Vernon McCasland and Walter Sikes, instead of returning to ACC after earning their doctorates, went on to become leading biblical scholars for the Disciples of Christ. The event strengthened fundamentalist views and discouraged scholarly development within the churches of Christ.

> "Modernism is manism. Yes, I am a fundamentalist and glad of it. A preacher who is not a fundamentalist is not a servant of God."
> E. M. Borden, *Firm Foundation*, August 4, 1925, p. 3.

Modeled after the social gospel, A. M. Burton, owner of the Life and Casualty Insurance Company in Nashville, and E. H. Ijams, a professor at David Lipscomb College, launched in 1925 the Central Church of Christ's facility that provided shelter and employment for the homeless, medical and dental care for the poor, and food for the hungry.

Many congregations began adding Sunday school wings to buildings and introducing individual communion cups. The non-Sunday school and one-cup churches saw these innovations as signs of worldliness and broke away from the majority. While the mainstream had divided opinions over pacifism in the wake of World War I, the non-Sunday school churches under the leadership of the *Apostolic Way* maintained a strong pacifist position.

During this time, preaching over the radio became common. Fred Little became the first preacher of the churches of Christ to preach over the radio in March 1922. By the late 1920s, A. M. Burton bought radio station WLAC. Burton sponsored so many radio programs by the Central Church of Christ and other congregations that the station call letters became known as "We Love All Campbellites."

With increasing wealth and influence, congregations and preachers began to become active in social and political issues. Nashville congregations used the Hardeman Tabernacle sermons to show that the churches of Christ were a new social and political force in the South. For example, A. B. Barret's lobbying efforts

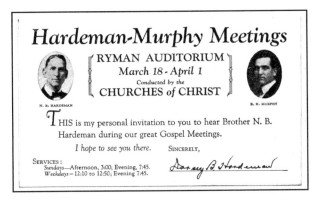

Card distributed door-to-door to advertise the 1928 "Tabernacle Meeting," with Hardeman speaking and B. H. Murphy as song leader

Person of the Decade:
N. B. Hardeman

Hardeman (1874-1965), who turned 50 in 1924, was at the peak of his career during this decade. Hardeman held three of his five defining gospel meetings in Nashville in 1922, 1923, and 1928, better known as the Hardeman Tabernacle Sermon series. The campaigns were modeled after the revivals of Billy Sunday and Sam Jones that also were conducted in the famous Ryman auditorium. The highly successful publicity for the Tabernacle sermon series gave the churches of Christ high visibility in the South. In the first series, Hardeman built common ground with his audience by stressing the importance of the Bible, drawing from denominational fundamentalist sources. In the later series, he turned to issues of the church. However, Hardeman stated in the third series, "I have never been so egotistical to say that my brethren with whom I commune . . . are the *only* Christians on this earth. I never said that in my life. I do make the claim that we are Christians *only*." The Tabernacle sermons became models for similar efforts by G. C. Brewer and Foy E. Wallace, Jr. in the 1930s and 1940s, culminating in Jimmy Allen's famous campaigns in the 1960s. Hardeman also held the Hardeman-Boswell debate on instrumental music in Nashville in 1923. Hardeman, Vice President of Freed-Hardeman College until 1923, returned as President in 1925, staying in that position until 1950. Hardeman also was a highly successful evangelist, holding countless meetings across the U.S. in the 1920s.

to get Tennessee's anti-evolution legislation passed led to the famous Scopes Trial in 1925. Lew D. Hill, speaker of the Tennessee senate and a member of a congregation in Sparta, successfully led the effort to pass anti-evolution legislation. Similar successful efforts to pass anti-evolution laws in Oklahoma and Arkansas were supported by leading preachers. G. C. Brewer went on a 1927 preaching tour to major cities featuring a sermon against evolution. Brewer received the support of Baptist minister J. Frank Norris and other fundamentalist preachers and advertised himself as the "Bryan of the Southwest." Unfortunately, some members were attracted to the Ku Klux Klan. For example, J. D. Tant surprisingly defended the KKK saying, "I am doing all I can to help them and … if the K.K.K. will attend my meeting and add to the meager support my brethren have to give … I'll certainly accept their help."

KU KLUX KLAN: A racist political organization that defended the superiority of the white race and Protestant morality and opposed alcoholism, Catholics, and African-Americans.

Fundamentalist views of the Bible dominated, used by college presidents to appeal to parents to send their children to Christian colleges instead of state universities, which were suspected of being modernist. Inerrancy was used to keep Bible professors from holding divergent views. The Fundamentalist/Modernist controversy is discussed more fully beginning on p. 53.

Meanwhile, premillennial views spread slowly through the efforts of popular preacher and writer R. H. Boll. While organized opposition to Boll did not surface until the 1930s, some efforts occurred to marginalize Boll in the 1920s. Characterized by an increasing and interesting diversity throughout the 1920s, most within the churches of Christ were optimistic about the future on the eve of the Great Depression. This decade, overlooked by most Restoration historians, anticipated many of the problems and arguments that erupted later in the century.

- By Michael Casey

Cover of the "Fundamentals," a treatise on Fundamentalism by professors from schools including Moody Bible Institute, Chicago, and Southwestern Theological Seminary, Fort Worth, Texas

1920-1930
Fundamentalist Controversy

DISCUSSION QUESTIONS

1. Why would James A. Allen think that the Union Avenue church building was too extravagant?
2. Of all the ideas embraced by the churches of Christ in the 1920s, which ones do you think were the most significant? Why?
3. What topics of controversy would have been best for churches of Christ to avoid? Why?

CHALLENGE QUESTIONS

1. N. B. Hardeman borrowed methods from the revivalists of his day. When is it appropriate to borrow methods from the wider religious world today?
2. Many leading preachers of the 1920s became entangled in the leading political issues of the time. When should Christians be involved in political issues? When should they avoid getting involved in politics?
3. In the 1920s, many churches eagerly embraced and used the new technology of radio. What new technologies should the church use today? Why? Which ones should be avoided? Why?

Sunlight illumines the Central Church of Christ, Nashville, Tennessee and its congregation in 1925, the year of its founding

1930-1940

BEGINNING OF THE END OF PREMILLENNIALISM

"Churches of Christ, as I had observed them during the first quarter of the 20th century, were commendably strong in doctrine, but were often very, very weak in good works."
- **E. H. IJAMS,** *co-founder of the Central Church of Christ, Nashville, Tennessee*

CHURCHES of Christ faced continuing challenges in the 1930s. As the decade opened, they struggled over the division from the Christian Church and responded by planting new congregations and constructing small buildings. Few congregations, even in the cities, had more than 150 members.

Certain key persons moved from one group to another. For example, Hall Calhoun (1863-1935), who had received a Ph.D. in New Testament from Harvard in 1904, succeeded J. W. McGarvey at the College of Bible in Lexington, Kentucky; later, however, Calhoun departed from the Christian Church in the middle 1920s, taught at Freed-Hardeman, and then preached in Nashville.

PREMILLENNIALISM: The view that Christ will return to earth to set up a kingdom that will last for a thousand years. Premillennialism is contrasted to "amillennialism," that is, the belief that Christ will not reign on the earth for a thousand years.

Preachers combated Evolution, Modernism, Biblical criticism, Communism and, toward the end of the decade, Premillennialism. The role of grace in salvation also came to the forefront as the result of books published by K. C. Moser (1893-1976). G. C. Brewer defended the views of Moser while Foy E. Wallace, Jr. and many others questioned them.

The decade of the 1930s was a period of growth, especially in the region of strength for churches of Christ, 200 miles on each side of a line running from Pittsburgh to El Paso. *The Gospel Advocate* and *Firm Foundation* both reported about 14,000 baptisms a year in the 1930s, according to Robert Hooper in *A Distinct People.*

The main evangelistic thrust was the gospel meeting. Every church, large and small, and every preacher held gospel meetings. Many churches were planted through a meeting held in a new location or town. A typical gospel meeting ran two weeks, spanning three Sundays, though some were longer. Gospel meetings, especially in the summer, were held in the open air, or in a tent, normally commencing about dusk.

As the meeting opened, the sermons focused on the identity, name, and organization of the church. The sermons for the remainder of the first week included ways of interpreting the Bible, the work of the Holy Spirit, and music in the assembly. In the second week, the sermons centered on the gospel plan of salvation: hearing, believing, confessing, repenting, and being baptized. The climax came with a sermon on hell and eternal damnation. In some congregations, sermons were also preached in the morning, focusing upon the work of the church, devotional items, and Christian living.

The 1930s were depression years. Church people across the land did what they could to help the needy, from making quilts and clothing to supplying fresh garden produce and canned fruits and vegetables for later consumption. Some churches undertook major assistance programs, including the Central Church of Christ in Nashville and the Oak Cliff Church of Christ in Dallas.

The leaders in the Central church were E. H. Ijams, a respected preacher and educator; A. M. Burton, founder and president of the Life and Casualty Insurance

E. H. Ijams, respected educator and minister, at a residence for homeless or destitute young men sponsored by the Central church, Nashville, Tennessee, during the Great Depression

Beginning of the End of Premillennialism   63

Event of the Decade:
Foy E. Wallace Jr. Appointed
Editor of the *Gospel Advocate*

The appointment of Foy E. Wallace, Jr. (1896-1979), a Texan, to the editorship of the *Gospel Advocate* (1930-1934) was the key event of the 1930s. (Go to http://www.bible.acu.edu/Stone-Campbell for resources, texts, and links about the Stone-Campbell Movement.) The leading predecessors of Wallace were millennialists of some sort: Thomas and Alexander Campbell, Barton W. Stone, and Walter Scott all had favored either post-millennialism, or an incipient premillennialism; David Lipscomb, James A. Harding, J. N. Armstrong, and R. C. Bell were premillennialists, though they spoke little about it; R. H. Boll (1875-1956), front-page editor for the *Gospel Advocate* from 1909-1915, had advocated a more detailed and aggressive premillennialism, one that focused on an increase of evil and the resultant necessity of the in-breaking of God. He also was much more grace-oriented and less critical of those not claiming membership in the churches of Christ. Foy E. Wallace, Jr. took up the gauntlet against premillennialism, first in the *Gospel Advocate* and, later in the decade, in the *Gospel Guardian* and the *Bible Banner*. By the 1940s, mainstream churches of Christ were essentially amillennial, and the premillennialists became more and more a distinct, if not separate, group within churches of Christ. The shift toward amillennialism had been occurring for some time. Emphasis was given to the role of humans in planting and building churches. The church, it was argued, is the kingdom of God on earth. Not only does the church nurture purity, but its influence would spill over into communities and ultimately the nation. It would be through human effort that these changes would occur, they believed, not so much the in-breaking of God into history. History would end with the coming again of Jesus Christ.

Company; and E. W. McMillan, the church's minister from 1938-41. This Nashville congregation commenced the decade with 576 members, exploding by 1941 to 1,200 members. The congregation initiated a medical and dental clinic with the work donated by doctors and dentists in the congregation. Central also had classes in Bible, personal hygiene, dietetics, and health, according to Harold Shank in *Restoration Quarterly* (1999). In addition, Central launched programs for visiting the sick, supplying funds for rent, burials, bus fare, transportation, clothing, groceries, and coal. The church offered a free noon meal to the homeless and poor, and it helped people find jobs.

THE SOCIAL GOSPEL:
From 1880, an American liberal view that the church should focus on social causes to bring the kingdom of Christ to earth.

They had two living facilities, one housing 110 women and another 60 men.

The 1,000-member Oak Cliff congregation in Dallas, with W. L. Oliphant as the minister, especially focused on the poor. As the depression wore on, Dallas County got into financial trouble and was no longer able to assist the needy. So county officials sent out letters to 800 churches in the County, asking them to support whatever number of poor families they could. Wyatt Sawyer, a member at Oak Cliff, reported that Oak Cliff accepted 38 families from the list, while continuing to do whatever they could to help other needy persons.

Despite controversies, the churches in the 1930s planted numerous churches both in the United States and in foreign countries. Congregations and members also supplied the needs of many who were in financial difficulty.

- By Thomas Olbricht

Person of the Decade:
G. C. Brewer
(1884-1956)

Grover Cleveland Brewer was at his peak in the 1930s. A vigorous speaker and debater, with an inexhaustible energy that touched on almost every facet of church life, he was an early proponent of congregational development. He favored "located" preachers and large congregations. He promoted church bulletins, membership lists and directories, church budgets, pledging, and multiple cups for communion. He favored large mission programs with congregational cooperation, and church support of Christian colleges. He published these views often in books, tracts, and religious journals.

Brewer was born in Giles County, Tennessee. He first attended Johnson Bible College in Knoxville, Tennessee, but he completed his classroom education at Nashville Bible School (now Lipscomb University), graduating in 1911. He preached for large churches in Tennessee, Los Angeles, and Texas, including Broadway Church of Christ in Lubbock.

In the 1930s, Brewer spoke and debated in Fundamentalist as well as churches of Christ circles on the issues of evolution, prohibition, communism, and Catholicism. Brewer was a consummate orator with a sonorous, but sometimes gruff, voice.

AMERICAN FUNDAMENTALISM: From 1910 focused on Biblical inerrancy, the virgin birth, the sacrificial atonement, Christ's bodily resurrection, performance of miracles, and the premillennial reign of Christ.

Noted for rigor of argument and the marshaling of biblical texts and contemporary data, his preaching heralded salvation by grace and the non-denominational character of Christianity. He questioned the crusade of Foy E. Wallace, Jr. against premillennialism, even though he declared himself an amillennialist. Brewer wrote of his life's work in two books: *Forty Years on the Firing Line* (1948) and *A Story of Toil and Tears, of Love and Laughter: Being the Autobiography of G. C. Brewer* (1957).

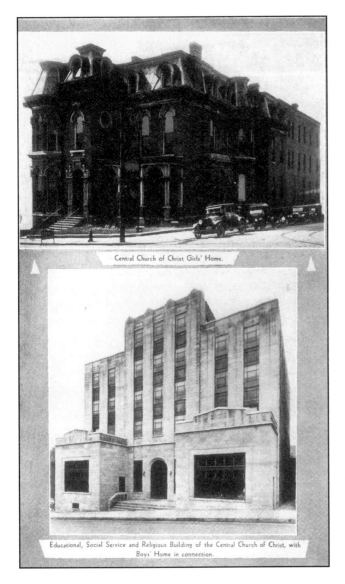

Central Church of Christ Girls' Home.

Educational, Social Service and Religious Building of the Central Church of Christ, with Boys' Home in connection.

Two buildings of the Central Church, Nashville, Tennessee during the Great Depression. One building was a residence for homeless young women, the other an educational and social service building of the church.

Russell Street Church of Christ, Nashville, Tennessee, September 1935

1930-1940
Beginning of the End of Premillennialism

DISCUSSION QUESTIONS

1. What were the major developments in churches of Christ in the 1930s?
2. How did the Great Depression influence church and members' activities? How did the move toward the Social Gospel occur?
3. What sort of millennialists were James A. Harding, Alexander Campbell, R. H. Boll, and Foy E. Wallace, Jr.? Each of these four held a different viewpoint. Why did the amillennial approach prevail at the end of the 1930s?

CHALLENGE QUESTIONS

1. In what ways did G. C. Brewer change the manner in which churches operated?
2. In what ways were outlooks in churches of Christ in this decade similar to and different from those of the American Fundamentalists?

German Christians during the post-war period

1940-1950

POST-WWII EVANGELISM

"[Following] … the Japanese attack on Pearl Harbor … millions of Americans were fighting around the globe. Christians [abroad] saw the great need—spiritual and material —and decided to do something about it."
-REINER KALLUS, *Munich, Germany*

NO decade since the 1860s influenced American life and thought as profoundly as that of the 1940s. Though churches of Christ had emerged as a distinct group at the beginning of the twentieth century, it was in this decade that we began to take on national stature and an international presence. Perhaps inevitably, World War II and its aftermath shaped every event of the decade in fundamental and complex ways.

Pacifism in churches of Christ, though severely tested in World War I, still had defenders like Ira Y. Rice, B. C. Goodpasture, and Jimmy Lovell. As World War II began, historic peace churches like the Mennonites and Brethren organized the "National Service Board for Religious Objectors" to administer alternative service centers for conscientious objectors. Many in churches of Christ regarded COs as cowards. Though Leslie G. Thomas represented churches of Christ on the Board, our congregations provided almost no funding for the 200 men from our congregations who served in these camps. The surge of patriotism following Pearl Harbor dealt our pacifist tradition a near fatal blow.

(continued on page 75)

Event of the Decade:
Post-WWII Missions

"We must work unrelentingly through our government for our rights as American citizens, but the most important thing is to pray fervently to the Lord of Harvest about the work and workers in the fields."

OLAN HICKS in a *Christian Chronicle* editorial, January 4, 1950, with reference to American missionaries in Italy who were being suppressed by the Italian government and the Roman Catholic Church, an incident that ultimately caused then-Senator Lyndon B. Johnson and the State Department to protest to the Italian government over treatment of missionaries.

World War II served as a catalyst to spur churches of Christ into unprecedented mission efforts. As early as 1943, G. C. Brewer, then at the Broadway Church in Lubbock, called for a massive effort to evangelize Europe and Asia at the war's end. Brewer's successor, M. Norvel Young, proposed a plan of "sponsoring churches" for cooperating in specific efforts.

Broadway called a meeting in 1946 to promote European missions and sent Otis Gatewood and Roy Palmer to Frankfurt the next year. Others entered Germany after a second meeting in 1948. By the end of the decade, nine German congregations had been established.

The Union Avenue church in Memphis took special interest in the Japanese work, supporting E. W. McMillan to conduct evangelistic meetings, start an orphanage, and serve as the first president of Ibaraki Christian College, established in 1948. By 1949, nineteen congregations had been established and more than 1,500 baptized.

Mission work in Italy began after a survey trip by Cline Paden and Bill Hatcher in late 1947. The Crescent Hill church in Brownfield, Texas, Paden's sponsor, promoted the Italian work.

Mission work by churches of Christ grew in other parts of Europe and Asia, as well as in Latin America and Africa in the post-war era. The number of missionaries increased from 46 in 1946 to around 200 in 1950, a figure that would continue to grow through the next two decades.

Otis Gatewood (1911-1999) became synonymous with world missions in Churches of Christ over the course of his life. First a missionary to New Mexico and Utah, following World War II he pioneered evangelism in Germany, Austria, and the Iron Curtain countries—helping to evangelize 55 nations—and served also as president of Michigan Christian College and European Christian College.

E. W. McMillan served as president of Ibaraki Christian College, Japan

Jack Nadeau, missionary, speaking at the church of Christ in Munich, Germany. The post-WWII environment lent itself to an unprecedented number of mission efforts.

The distinguished service of African-Americans during World War II highlighted another national issue plaguing churches of Christ—racial discrimination. In churches of Christ, as in most religious bodies in the country, paternalism marked the relationship between black and white congregations. White benefactors supported preachers like Marshall Keeble, and white churches made sure their black brothers and sisters had separate places to worship. As the Roosevelt administration began to act against racial injustice, African-American churches of Christ created structures for doing their work in a segregated nation and church. In 1941, they founded the Nashville Christian Institute. The next year G. P. Bowser published the first National Directory of Churches of Christ, Colored,

"I hope and pray that the day will come when we all can see this school headed by Brother McMillan and also endorsed by Dr. Young as the chairman of the Board of Directors, one of the greatest colleges in the world, educating boys and girls of the Negro race and preparing them to get out and meet anybody that rises up against the church of Christ."

-MARSHALL KEEBLE, "The Church Among the Colored," 1950 Abilene Christian College Lectures

promoting a solid identity among those congregations. In 1945, African-American churches[1] began the annual National Lectureship and, by the end of the decade, established Southwestern Christian College in Terrell, Texas. While these efforts empowered members of black churches of Christ to work together in the midst of a sinfully segregated society, yet the efforts created structures that today perpetuate the existence of two separate bodies.

Soldiers from churches of Christ serving in World War II were deeply affected by the need for evangelism and benevolent assistance in Europe and Asia. In 1946, the Broadway church in Lubbock, Texas called a national meeting to discuss missions

---

[1] Web Resource: http://www.mun.ca/rels/restmov/subs/race.html Race and the Church of Christ. Documents compiled by Don Haymes on the Restoration Movement site of Hans Rollmann.

SPONSORING CHURCH: Arrangement where the elders of one congregation direct a mission or ministry effort, receiving and administering funds from other congregations. The method avoided establishing extra-congregational organizations like the missionary society.

cooperation. A sensitive issue since the mid-1800s, cooperation took on a new hue in the aftermath of World War II and the increasing confidence and affluence of churches of Christ. Broadway became a "sponsoring church" for the work in Germany, Union Avenue in Memphis did the same for Japan, and Crescent Hill in Brownfield, Texas supported the work in Italy. Some saw such moves as evidence of growing institutionalism and modernism in churches of Christ, a concern that would lead in the next decade to an open break.

Churches of Christ experienced a growing self-confidence in other ways as well. In 1943, Olan Hicks established *The Christian Chronicle* as a communion-wide newspaper focused on missions. The post-war influx of students under the G.I. Bill of Rights brought exponential growth to our existing colleges and aided the success of new ones, including Montgomery Bible School (Alabama Christian) in 1942, Florida Christian in 1946, and Columbia Christian in 1948. This growth and an increased desire for trained ministers moved the colleges to seek regional accreditation. Though only Pepperdine had achieved it by the end of the decade, Abilene Christian, under Don Morris (president from 1940-1969), was not far behind.

INSTITUTIONALISM: The creation of institutions to perform ministry and missions tasks apart from local congregations. Those who opposed organizations like Herald of Truth and orphan homes were labeled anti-institutional.

In 1946, M. I. Young, Broadway's preacher, conducted a census of churches of Christ for the Federal Council of Churches' national directory. In significant ways, the decade signaled that churches of Christ were coming of age.

- By Douglas A. Foster

E. W. McMillan, missionaries, and Japanese leaders involved in the early days of Ibaraki Christian College

Person of the Decade:
Marshall Keeble, Who Spanned Two Decades, Influenced Two Worlds

While it could be argued that Marshall Keeble (1878-1968) reached the height of his long evangelistic career in the previous decade, he was by the 1940s one of the most widely-known and influential African-American leaders in churches of Christ. Keeble's preaching had been supported since the 1920s by A. M. Burton, owner of the Life and Casualty Insurance Company in Nashville, Tenn. Named President of Nashville Christian Institute (1941-1967) three years after its opening, Keeble funneled all fees from his widespread speaking engagements directly to the school.

Many both inside and outside black churches of Christ regarded Keeble as too accommodating to the church's white leadership. Many whites pointed to Keeble as the kind of humble leader blacks should imitate. Even his roles as school president and editor were largely controlled by whites. The evidence is clear, however, that Keeble's training[2] of scores of young preachers at NCI involved a complex approach to the realities of racial discrimination in society and church. From under his tutelage emerged leaders like Civil Rights lawyer Fred Gray and activist Floyd Rose.

Keeble's style was a mixture of folksy wit and pointed teaching. Four books, two doctoral dissertations, and two phonograph recordings provide a glimpse of the rich flavor of his teachings. Keeble connected with his audiences at a remarkable level, baptizing thousands in the United States and Africa.

---

[2] Web Resource: http://www.mun.ca/rels/restmov/people/mkeeble.html Articles by Marshall Keeble, as well as a recording of Keeble extending the invitation.

1940-1950
Post-WWII Evangelism

DISCUSSION QUESTIONS

1. In what ways was World War II a major influence on events and trends in churches of Christ in the 1940s?
2. What structures did black churches of Christ create in the 1940s that helped give them a clear identity separate from the white churches? How did these structures parallel those in the white churches?
3. What effect did the post-World War II boom have on educational institutions in churches of Christ? What effect did it have on the number of college-trained ministers?

CHALLENGE QUESTIONS

1. How do you regard the pacifists[3] and conscientious objectors in churches of Christ during World War II? Do you know anyone who takes a pacifist position today? Why do you think most of the early leaders of the Stone-Campbell Restoration Movement were pacifists?
2. Those who opposed the "sponsoring church" method of doing mission work claimed it was wrong for the same reasons the missionary society in the 19th century was wrong. Compare the 19th-century missionary society with the 20th-century sponsoring church approach. How are they alike? How are they different? How important is the method of evangelization if Christ is preached?
3. Why did churches of Christ maintain a strictly segregated existence in the 20th century? How was segregation justified? Was such division simply unavoidable in that earlier time? What could members of churches of Christ have done in the era of segregation to fight against such sin and injustice?

---

[3] Web Resource: http://www.mun.ca/rels/restmov/subs/peace.html Peace issues; several documents illustrating pacifist sentiment in churches of Christ.

A 1950s home Bible Study scene used in advertising for the Jule Miller filmstrips

1950-1960

'NON-INSTITUTIONAL' SPLIT

"The church of Christ must possess something which no other church can claim for many to forsake their former teaching and associates and cleave to a different doctrine and a new people. That 'something' is the doctrine of Christ."
- THOMAS L. CAMPBELL, *Introduction,* Why I Left *(1949)*

THE post-war, G.I. generation energized the churches of Christ in the 1950s for growth, international expansion, and an accumulation of unprecedented material assets.

Missions were at the forefront of news as the decade opened. Through the decade, *The Christian Chronicle* gave an international flavor to the church as each issue carried front-page news about missionaries on every continent.

In 1951, *The Yearbook of American Churches* reported 17,500 churches and two million members, supporting claims that the churches of Christ were the fastest-growing religious body in America.

"Personal work" programs, using the Jule Miller filmstrip and recorded narrative, gave ordinary church members an attractively packaged plan of salvation to take

COTTAGE MEETINGS: The term used to describe taking the Jule Miller filmstrips, Tisdale charts, or other aids into the setting of a neighbor's home and showing a family or group information related to the plan of salvation, often resulting in conversions.

(continued on page 84)

Event of the Decade:
'Non-Institutional' Split

"Who knows who shall hear? It may be a clerk in a dime store, or possibly a tired, exhausted businessman, or maybe even a Senator of the United States. In any case, this is our opportunity to preach the gospel where it has never been preached before. Pray that we may not fail. Pray that those who have the financial means of making it possible may not fail." BATSELL BARRETT BAXTER, commenting on goals to expand Herald of Truth radio and television broadcasting to over 1,100 stations, reaching a potential audience of 100 million persons. *Christian Chronicle*, December 22, 1959.

Though the "non-institutional" or "anti-cooperation" controversy was more philosophically and theologically complex than it may now seem, its 1950s result was the emergence of a minority in churches of Christ holding to the Restoration Movement's concepts of rigid congregational autonomy, while a vast majority of churches agreed to the concept of multiple churches financing causes organized, usually called "sponsored," by single congregations. The central question was whether or not, scripturally, churches could cooperate in funding activities led either by a single church or an extra-church organization.

The controversy had gained energy in the late 1940s, as some Christian colleges asked for help from local churches. Opposition to a plan, organized by the Broadway church in Lubbock, for a post-war effort in Europe came from Roy Cogdill and Fanning Yater Tant, whose *Gospel Guardian* became the medium for dissent in 1949. By 1951, the church divided in Lufkin, Texas, as Cogdill and Cled Wallace took opposing positions. When the *Gospel Advocate* criticized the Cogdill faction, a battle of words then began between the *Advocate* and the *Guardian,* leading to a 1954 *Advocate* call to "quarantine" the "anti-cooperation" wing.

Positions hardened as cooperative causes grew to include the support of orphan homes and The Herald of Truth broadcast. Herald of Truth's E. R. Harper debated Tant, and Guy N. Woods debated Cogdill; and the ultimate result was as many as 2,000 congregations subscribed to the "non-institutional" position.

The GOSPEL GUARDIAN

Dedicated to the Propagation and Defense of New Testament Christianity

VOLUME 3   MAY 3, 1951   NUMBER 1

THE ISSUE OF INSTITUTIONALISM -- No. 1

Bryan Vinson, Dallas, Texas

To institute is to set up; originate, and establish; found; organize; hence, to set on foot. An institution, therefore, would be that which is established and organized. Institutionalism is defined as "the upholding of institutions, of their usefulness, validity, or, in the case of established institutions, of their authority and sanctity."

The issue of institutionalism would necessarily involve either the discussion of the usefulness and validity of a proposed establishment, or the inauguration of an organization, or the authority and sanctity of an existing one. Unfortunately, the first of these courses is rarely, if ever, pursued; ordinarily, men first foster and set in operation some pet project without a prior testing of the scriptural validity for it, and only afterwards (when and if it is challenged) attempt a belated defense of it. Frequently even that defense is lacking, and those questioning the scriptural authority of the organization are either ignored or classed as cranks and trouble-makers. Such a course is not only unmanly, but, when eternally evaluated, is disastrously ruinous and constitutes a flagrant disregard of the apostolic injunction to "Prove all things and hold fast that which is good."

Current Discussions

It is to be fervently hoped that the current discussions on this subject, as it relates to colleges and the formulated programs for preaching the gospel in foreign lands, shall stimulate the brethren generally to think through to a proper and safe position. Especially is there a need for a thorough study of the church in relation to its obligation to the needy and how that responsibility can be scripturally discharged. To such an end are these lines being written. There is certainly no desire to foment any kind of strife, nor to say one single word that will discourage any Christian or congregation from doing the right thing, but rather the desire is to provoke a greater interest in determining exactly what the will of the Lord is, to the end that it can be more acceptably performed.

There are a number of orphan homes now operating under the claimed "auspices" of the church of Christ, and the number seems to be increasing rapidly. The nature of the appeal made by these homes, and the power of their influence, stems from the sympathy which every normal persons feels for the unfortunate. Here, indeed, is a challenge to the generosity of the saints. The potency of the appeal is evidenced by the very general and well nigh universal response by the church in supporting such, and responding to the calls for help. The churches are told that such assistance is the work of the church; and that a failure to respond constitutes a breach of our divinely imposed obligation. Also, (in some instances at least) the world is solicited for support. Business firms, civic orders, and women's social clubs are appealed to. A strange and inconsistent procedure if these institutions are truly the work of the church! Why is the world's support sought and secured for these homes if they are indeed "the work of the church?" If it is the obligation of the Lord's church to establish, maintain, and support such homes, how can anybody justify the practice of appealing to the world for support? I am sincerely interested in an answer to this question.

Papistical Philosophy

The general acceptance which is accorded these institutions by the church is predicated on a papistical philosophy. This may be noted in these particulars:

1. Traditional. We know that with the Catholics tradition is invested with greater authority than the Scriptures. The term "tradition" simply denotes a giving over, a handing down. The merit or demerit attaching to any particular tradition depends on who delivered it, or who handed it down. The Jews made void the commandments of God by their traditions, and so have many others. The Catholics have surely done so in our day. Such weight given to tradition arises from the persuasion that what "my church" teaches and practices must be right, or else it would not be practiced and taught!

Such an attitude is, of course, gross assumption, and the very essence of sectarianism. It creates complacency and nurtures self-satisfaction in a state of religious inertia, regardless of how erroneous the position may be. The present generation of the Christian Church doubtless entertains no misgivings at all respecting the missionary societies and the organ. These things have become "traditional" with them, and are accepted without a moment's hesitation. But on the principle of "teaching no other doctrine" than that of the apostles, and an adherence to the rule of "doing Bible things in Bible ways" a complete repudiation of this mode or reasoning is required. Every

(See INSTITUTIONALISM Page 5)

"The Gospel Guardian," edited by Roy Cogdill and Fanning Yater Tant, opposed cooperative projects such as joint support of missionaries

into "cottage meetings." The Herald of Truth began national radio broadcasts in 1952 and expanded into television by 1954. V. E. Howard broadcast to a wide swath of the central United States from a super-powerful Mexican radio station.

Businesslike organization swept larger churches, complete with corporate flow charts and committees. Ira North's *You Can March for the Master* described evangelism through tightly-planned campaigns.

A construction boom created carefully-designed buildings, some seating more than 2,000, containing first-rate classrooms, kitchens, fellowship halls and, occasionally, recreational facilities. *The Church is Building* set total assets at more than $147 million in 1956.

A baby boom filled the classrooms, using Bible school materials and visual technologies produced by brotherhood firms. The Madison, Tennessee church promoted a national record of 3,000 in Bible school on a single Sunday. "Education directors" were appointed in some churches to supply, fill, and staff classrooms and to conduct large Vacation Bible Schools.

Eleven colleges were founded, seven surviving the century. Seventeen campus ministries, then called "Bible chairs," were established on state campuses. An annual national meeting of campus ministers (1957) and the *Campus Journal* (1958) were launched.

A band of (almost exclusively) men pursued doctorates at major universities, many returning to the growing church-related colleges. Harding (1952) and Abilene Christian (1953) joined Pepperdine in offering graduate Bible programs. A scholarly journal, *Restoration Quarterly*, began publication in 1957.

College lectureships and periodicals

"The church of Christ must possess something which no other church can claim for many to forsake their former teaching and associates and cleave to a different doctrine and a new people. That 'something' is the doctrine of Christ. If other religious bodies had 'it,' they, too, would be absorbed into the church of Christ." - THOMAS L. CAMPBELL
in the introduction to *Why I Left* (1949)

were at peak influence, helping create what was called a "brotherhood" identity and solidifying mainstream thought. Tens of thousands subscribed to the *Gospel Advocate, Firm Foundation, 20th Century Christian,* and *Power for Today.*

The church laid claim to an Olympic athlete, Bobby Morrow, and an entertainer, Pat Boone, and was proud to have a spot in American popular culture.

Churches of Christ remained racially segregated. The African-American church claimed about 1,000 churches and in 1950 founded a college in Terrell, Texas. Fred Gray, first trained as a preacher by Marshall Keeble, used his later legal training to defend Rosa Parks following the Montgomery Bus Boycott, a touchstone event that sparked the Civil Rights movement in 1955.

✳

MAINSTREAM OF CHURCHES OF CHRIST: The largest segment of churches of Christ that, until the 1960s, was especially served by two periodicals—the *Firm Foundation* and the *Gospel Advocate.*

Voice of Freedom was founded by G. C. Brewer in 1953 to combat Communism and Roman Catholicism. Some college programs heightened awareness of a Communist threat and promoted the "American way of life." Texas businessman H. L. Hunt sponsored minister Wayne Poucher in a national, daily, anti-communist broadcast called *Lifeline.*

In addition to the 1950s "anti-cooperation" break, seeds were sown for a kind of dissent that would shake the church in the 1960s. At the beginning of the decade, the book *Why I Left* contrasted the views of nine well-known preachers with their previously-held denominational beliefs, furthering the church's singular identity and helping solidify majority opinion. But by 1958, a different view was expressed when Margaret Edson O'Dowd published *In the Great Hand of God I Stand,* inspiring some who were critical of what they saw as the church's exclusivism, legalism, and lack of spirituality. Highly influential only in later decades, K. C. Moser's *The Gist of Romans* (1957) helped lay a foundation for theological shifts on grace, faith, and

"Dear God, I must find a way out. I am held as if by chains; by steel bands—chains of prejudiced people—bands of custom! ... Oh, God, my dear Father, give me the courage to find deliverance for myself—for my loved ones—for others."

MARGARET EDSON O'DOWD'S prayer, which she reported preceded her decision to abandon the churches of Christ in spite of her husband's (John O'Dowd) continuing as a preacher. *In the Great Hand of God I Stand* (1958), p. 30, and alluded to in her chapter in *Voices of Concern* (1966), pp. 144-53.

works, all positions that later would become mainstream.

Simmering outside the boundaries of mainstream consensus were W. Carl Ketcherside and Leroy Garrett who, though never leaving their clear anti-institutional and deeply autonomous tradition, began in the latter part of the decade to expound against what they saw as "sectarianism," "exclusivism," and "legalism" in the church. They emphasized what they believed was an ecumenical theme in the message of Alexander Campbell. Their platforms were the journals *Restoration Review* (Garrett, 1959) and *Mission Messenger* (Ketcherside, established much earlier but which began to discuss "exclusivism" in 1957). Many were confused upon seeing an ecumenical message emerging from the apparent right wing. Ketcherside and Garrett never renounced their anti-institutional position, but simply decided not to make it, along with many other issues, a "test of fellowship." Thousands of people subscribed to these two journals that expounded views outside the consensus but which have, nevertheless, influenced the shape of today's church.

End-of-the-decade issues of the *Christian Chronicle* revealed a greater focus on domestic evangelism and news from the colleges. Seventy-five prominent ministers' signatures appeared in the publication to support expansion of the Herald of Truth. Batsell Barrett Baxter was featured as the spokesman, both on radio and television, for his irenic approach to preaching the gospel to a nation moving away from its post-war religious fervor.

- By Steven Lemley

Person of the Decade:
M. Norvel Young
The Fellowship's 'Quintessential Builder'

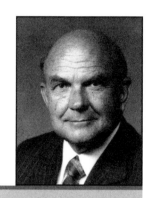

William Strauss and Neil Howe (*Generations,* 1991) wrote that those born between 1901 and 1924 comprised a unique group of "America's confident and rational problem solvers." Matt Norvel Young (1915-97) was perhaps the chief representative of his generation in our fellowship. Only 35 years old in 1950, his energy, intellect, interpersonal strengths, and devotion to worthy causes led to great contributions spanning six decades. Leaders found in him a confidant and advisor. In his lifetime, he moved between notable success, devastating personal failure, and back again, able to identify not only with some of the world's most visible and successful people, but also with the depths of human misery.

Founder and editor of *20th Century Christian* and *Power for Today,* prolific writer for other periodicals, pulpit minister for the largest congregation in the 1950s (Broadway, Lubbock), world traveler and encourager of missionary efforts, and proponent for modern church buildings, Young was also pivotal in forming the Children's Home of Lubbock, Lubbock Christian School, Lubbock Christian University, and in the 1970s, Pepperdine's Malibu campus. Richard Hughes calls him "the quintessential builder among Churches of Christ" (*Reviving the Ancient Faith,* 1996).

Educated at Lipscomb, Abilene Christian, Vanderbilt, and Peabody, Young developed a thoughtful, energetic, visionary, and optimistic preaching style in line with his personal character. He excelled as a peacemaker among brethren who were inclined to discord.

In 1957, he and wife, Helen, were called to Los Angeles where he served as president of Pepperdine University until 1971, where he is credited with saving the financially and philosophically troubled institution. He later was named Chancellor, serving as Chancellor Emeritus until his death in 1997.

1950-1960
'Non-Institutional' Split

DISCUSSION QUESTIONS

1. Why were evangelistic methods such as filmstrips and home meetings effective in the 1950s? Why are such methods not used often today? What has replaced the "cottage meeting?"
2. How might the 1950s emphasis on Sunday school attendance have been an important factor in church growth in that decade? What is the present status of Sunday school attendance in today's churches? Why?
3. What is the importance of the "non-institutional" split of the 50s to all churches of Christ today?

CHALLENGE QUESTIONS

1. Based on what you know and have read about the G.I. Generation (the "greatest generation"), what life experiences might have impacted their leadership of the churches of Christ in the 1950s? What aspects of that generation's influence remains among today's churches?
2. How do you think the pilgrimage of a significant number of church leaders to earn doctorates might have affected the church in the 1950s? How do you think it has affected the church since then? How might things be different if they had "stayed home?"
3. What has happened to the influence of periodicals and colleges on consensus within the churches of Christ? How and why do you think it is different from the 1950s? What, if anything, has taken their place?
4. How are racial distinctions within churches of Christ different today than you understand them to have been in the 1950s? In what ways do you see change? In what ways are things the same?

*John Allen Chalk
and Jim Bevis in a
worship service for
Campus Evangelism,
an evangelistic effort
that trained more
than 4,000 college
students for campus
outreach*

1960-1970

SPEECH QUESTIONS RACIAL ATTITUDES

"Who knows who shall hear? It may be a clerk in a dime store, possibly a tired, exhausted businessman, or maybe even a Senator of the United States. In any case, this is our opportunity to preach the gospel where it has never been preached before."
- BATSELL BARRETT BAXTER, *regarding the Herald of Truth*
(*The Christian Chronicle, December 22, 1959*)

THE decade of the 1960s stands as a major line of demarcation in the history of churches of Christ, both politically and theologically.

While churches of Christ had been moving to the right politically since the end of World War I, several factors in the 1960s pushed the mainstream of this tradition even further in that direction. First, churches of Christ joined hands with a variety of conservative Protestant groups in an effort to undermine the possible election of the Roman Catholic John F. Kennedy to the presidency of the United States. Second, the Vietnam War enhanced the anti-Communist stance that churches of Christ had cultivated for at least two decades. Third, the domestic protests against that war prompted churches of Christ to embrace a conservative, law-and-order posture toward social issues. And fourth, the racial crisis of the 1960s revealed the deep racial divide that had been growing within this fellowship for most of the 20th century.

Yet, the response to these crises was not as tidy as may appear at first glance, for by the time the decade had run its course, churches of Christ had undergone an

91

Event of the Decade:
Carl Spain's 1960 Lectureship Speech

The decade of the 1960s was less than two months old when Carl Spain, a gospel preacher and professor of Bible at Abilene Christian College, delivered a speech that would have such far-reaching repercussions that today, more than forty years later, we can safely regard it as the event of the decade.

Spain delivered this speech in the context of the Civil Rights Movement that had begun in 1955 when Rosa Parks refused to give up her seat on a bus to a white man in Montgomery, Alabama. In the years immediately following Parks' decisive action, churches of Christ did very little to combat racial discrimination within their own ranks.

Spain spoke during the annual ACC Lectureship in February of 1960, and he chose that occasion as his opportunity to condemn the racial segregation that plagued not only Abilene Christian College but also the entire fellowship of churches of Christ.

"God forbid," he thundered, "that churches of Christ, and schools operated by Christians, shall be the last stronghold of refuge for socially sick people who have Nazi illusions about the Master Race."

Spain's speech brought considerable pressure on Abilene Christian University and was at least partly responsible for the fact that the process of racial integration began at ACC the following year. Even then, however, progress was slow. But Carl Spain had unleashed among churches of Christ the power of the gospel, energy that would slowly drain the competing power of racial discrimination in this tradition.

"Marching under the standard of the god of mammon and bluffing his way with ballots and bullets, the white man put his big white foot on the Negro's neck, quoted the pledge of allegiance to the flag, and piously recited platitudes about all men being born free and equal."

−CARL SPAIN, "Modern Challenges to Christian Morals," 1960 Abilene Christian College lectureship.

unofficial, three-way split, most often understood in theological terms.

The progressives quarreled with the mainstream on a number of issues. First, they questioned the legitimacy of both the restoration principle and the traditional command-example-necessary inference hermeneutic. Second, deeply concerned as they were with social issues like the Vietnam War and the domestic racial crisis, many progressives found irrelevant the traditional debates that treated the Bible as a blueprint for worship and church organization.

Three new journals[1] emerged to serve the progressive wing of the movement. *Restoration Quarterly,* founded in 1957, served especially the interests of academics in the churches of Christ. Two popular journals — *Mission*, founded in 1967, and *Integrity*, founded in 1969 — addressed a wide range of issues, ranging from the hermeneutic crisis to urban decay to race to the Holy Spirit.

Conservatives responded with several new journals of their own, most notably *The First Century Christian*, established in 1967, and *The Spiritual Sword*, founded in 1969. In addition, as conservatives increasingly lost faith in church of Christ-related colleges to prepare men they judged suitable for the pulpit ministry, they established schools of preaching that offered training in Bible and related subjects but did little or nothing with the traditional liberal arts.

In the meantime, the mainstream of churches of Christ was forced to grapple with issues being raised by the broader culture on the one hand, and by progressives and conservatives in this tradition on the other. Soon, the mainstream found itself addressing three issues in particular: the relation of churches of Christ to believers in other Christian traditions, the role of the Holy Spirit in the lives of baptized believers, and the legitimacy of the traditional hermeneutic.

---

[1] Web Resource: www.mun.ca/rels/restmov Extensive site of resources and original texts of the American Restoration Movement.

*

George Phillip (G. P.) Bowser
(1874-1950)

P rominent preacher and educator among black churches of Christ during the first half of the 20th century, founded schools in Nashville and Silver Point, Tennessee; began the *Christian Echo* in 1902. In contrast to Marshall Keeble, he openly opposed racial discrimination.

[R. Vernon Boyd, *Undying Dedication: The Story of G. P. Bowser.* Nashville, TN: Gospel Advocate Co., 1985.]

When all was said and done, the 1960s brought to the mainstream of churches of Christ some significant changes. First, churches would increasingly abandon their traditional sectarian posture vis-à-vis other Christian traditions and would inch their way ever closer toward a niche in the American evangelical mosaic. By the dawn of the 21st century, many congregations of churches of Christ had embraced an evangelical understanding of the Christian faith and an evangelical style of worship.

HERMENEUTIC: The principles that govern how one reads a text—in this case, the Bible. The traditional hermeneutic for churches of Christ has been "direct command, approved example, and necessary inference."

Second, beginning in the 1960s, the traditional hermeneutic, grounded as it was in the eighteenth-century Enlightenment, would slowly lose its near-universal hold on this tradition. The rise of postmodernism in the larger culture later would only hasten this transition.

And third, members of churches of Christ would become significantly more receptive to the power of the Holy Spirit, both in conversion and in the lives of believers. By the dawn of the 21st century, many members of churches of Christ embraced the indwelling Holy Spirit with considerable zeal and seemed to have no awareness that the role of the Spirit was ever even contested among Christians in this tradition.

- By Richard T. Hughes

Person of the Decade:
Batsell Barrett Baxter:
Speaker to the Nation

Optimism was alive among churches of Christ in the 1950s. Among those men who gave leadership to this optimism was Batsell Barrett Baxter. Born in 1916, Baxter received much of his education during the Great Depression. Educated at David Lipscomb College (now Lipscomb University) and Abilene Christian, he received his Ph.D at the University of Southern California in Speech. His education in speech led him to both preaching and teaching, first at Pepperdine College and, beginning in 1945, to a long-term commitment to David Lipscomb College.

At Lipscomb, he taught speech with Carroll Ellis and Ira North. These three men educated a generation of preachers in a new and different delivery style. Mostly, the young men (including the writer of this essay) accepted Baxter's style as a standard. They went everywhere preaching the old gospel clothed in the new Baxter technique.

Preaching was the passion of Baxter's life. In Nashville, he preached for the Hillsboro Church of Christ, becoming one of the best-known preachers among churches of Christ. He would hold the Hillsboro pulpit from 1951 until his death in 1982. Equally important, he was a regular at college lectureships and, when area-wide meetings became popular in the 1950s and the 1960s, Baxter preached in a number of them as well.

In 1959, the Highland Church of Abilene, Texas appointed Baxter speaker on its nation-wide Herald of Truth television program. Dan Harless, co-worker at Hillsboro, said of Baxter: "He has in his voice the quality of quiet urgency which I think is unsurpassed in the ministry today."

More than 150 television stations carried Baxter's message. By 1965, Herald of Truth and Baxter were synonymous. He truly was "speaker to the nation."

- By Robert E. Hooper

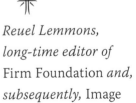

Reuel Lemmons,
long-time editor of
Firm Foundation *and,*
subsequently, Image
Magazine

John Allen Chalk's role as a "Herald of Truth" speaker during the 1960s made a significant contribution to race relations in our fellowship, says author Richard Hughes in Reviving the Ancient Faith

1960-1970
Speech Questions Racial Attitudes

DISCUSSION QUESTIONS

1. In what ways did churches of Christ move toward the right politically during the 1960s? Why?
2. Explain the nature of the three-way split that occurred within churches of Christ during the 1960s.
3. Who was Carl Spain? What was the heart of Carl Spain's speech at the Abilene Christian College lectureship in 1960? What were the repercussions of that speech?

CHALLENGE QUESTIONS

1. In what ways have churches of Christ become a part of the "evangelical mosaic" since the 1960s?
2. Ask members of your group to reminisce if any remembers Batsell Barrett Baxter. What characteristics made him unique? How did he connect with the spirit of his times?
3. How are race relations in the churches of Christ today? What, if any, will be the next important issue that may threaten to divide the churches?

A scene from an early workshop at International Bible College, Florence, Alabama. The IBC event was the catalyst for the widespread 1970s workshop movement. IBC is now Heritage Christian University.

1970-1980

THE SOUL-WINNING WORKSHOPS

"As time went on, increasing numbers of these young people abandoned Churches of Christ for other more socially concerned, more ecumenical, or more spirit-filled Christian traditions ... By the early 1970s, this exodus had become a significant concern."
-RICHARD T. HUGHES, Reviving the Ancient Faith, *p. 349*

THOUGH the foreshortening of historical perspective makes objective and accurate analysis of this period difficult, the 1970s might be characterized as paradoxical. While evangelism was the emphasis, decline was the reality.

From 1945-65, churches of Christ were one of the fifteen fastest-growing churches in America. The growth rate slowed, however, from 1965-73, reaching zero growth by the end of the 70s decade. But amazingly, the story of the 70s is largely one of evangelistic emphasis.

This decade also saw the fading of both the traditional gospel meeting and the "big name preachers" so often associated with those meetings. In their place emerged a whole new bevy of evangelistic approaches, including soul-winning workshops, World Bible School, television, the discipling movement at Crossroads and Boston, bus evangelism, Christian college campaigns, crusade campaigns in African-American churches, and the beginning of new preacher-training schools.

Soul-winning workshops and special needs seminars, ones on marriage in

TULSA WORKSHOP: The Tulsa International Soul-Winning Workshop began in 1975 and continues to operate. Go to www.tulsaworkshop.org for more information.

particular, took the place of many gospel meetings. Though these were often billed as evangelistic, they were a new genre of offerings in churches of Christ. The Brecheen-Faulkner Marriage Enrichment Seminars, which began in 1974, spawned a host of seminars for churches on marriage, family, and other contemporary topics.

Multiple-staff churches emerged as new areas of focus, such as youth ministry, were identified.

Mission Magazine (1967), *Spiritual Sword* (1969), and *Contending for the Faith* (1970) signaled the developing diversity, if not polarity, of the fellowship. The often-predicted split in the fellowship never occurred; instead, the fellowship manifested an ever-increasing diversity. The Pepperdine Lectureship gradually became the forum for diversity, while the Tulsa Workshop became the forum for evangelism.

Church statistician Flavil Yeakley (Searcy, Arkansas) reports that from 1965-73 churches of Christ continued to grow, but in 1973 membership began to decline at a one-third percent per year rate until it reached zero growth in 1980, where growth has remained plateaued since.

Batsell Barrett Baxter's off-the-record "Crisis" speech, in 1976 to a Herald of Truth workshop, cites Yeakley's charting of the precipitous drop in the growth rate from the fast growth years of 1945-65. Not only did Baxter note the problem, but he laid out the challenge.

Soul-winning workshops were a grassroots movement that began by addressing the needs of rank-and-file members by providing motivation and

www.worldbibleschool.net Begun in the 1950s by Jimmy Lovell, World Bible School now serves more than 2 million students in more than 140 nations. WBS is a non-profit organization located in Cedar Park, Texas and is directed by Tex Williams.

how-to skills for lay-member evangelism. Jimmy Lovell began World Bible School in the early 1970s as a means of spreading the gospel. Using the time and ability of myriads of lay teachers in congregations everywhere, literally thousands of students were soon teaching WBS Bible correspondence courses, producing converts mostly beyond the United States. Lay leaders provided much of the leadership in other evangelistic efforts as well, as church leaders were too often bogged down in issues and controversies.

- By Lynn A. McMillon

Event of the Decade:
Soul-Winning Workshops a Nationwide, Grassroots Movement

The soul-winning workshops began as the brainchild of Alan Bryan (pictured) in 1972 at International Bible College — with more than 3,000 attending a layman's hands-on workshop. By 1979, there were more than 30 of these special workshops and more than 300,000 people had attended them, a number far greater than the college lectureships. Marvin Phillips and Terry Rush led the Tulsa Workshop, which began in 1976 with 9,000 attendees, and grew to a high of 15,000 in 1978, drawing from 45 states and 20 countries. Attendance at Tulsa still averages around 12,000 every year.

For several years, soul-winning workshops were conducted in Indianapolis, Pensacola, Orlando, St. Louis, Seattle, San Antonio, Chattanooga, Denver, Ft. Wayne, Pueblo, Houston, and a dozen other cities. Alan Bryan provided significant influence, motivation, and consultation in the development of many of them.

The workshop movement attracted primarily church members interested in evangelism and special-needs topics rather than leaders and preachers interested in issue-oriented programs.

Minister Ira North teaches the "Amazing Grace Bible Class," videotaped in color on Wednesday night and telecast at 8:00 A.M. the following Sunday over WSIX-TX in Nashville. The class is conducted in the 3,000-seat auditorium of the Madison, Tennessee Church of Christ.

Person of the Decade:
Ira North, 'Mr. Enthusiasm,'
Sets the Standard at Madison

Ira North (1922-84) began to preach for the Madison, Tennessee congregation in 1952 and by the 1960s it was the largest congregation in the brotherhood. North was positive, faithful to God's word, and a tireless worker in encouraging church growth. He was enthusiastic about the church and reaching out to others, even stressing efficiency to a level some considered bordering on the overzealous.

"I have come to the conclusion that there is a key word in church growth if it is solid, stable and lasting. That key word is *balance*." IRA NORTH, "Balance: A Tried and Tested Formula for Church Growth," *Gospel Advocate*, 1983.

His slogan, "If you go they will come," reflected his philosophy of building the church through one-on-one evangelism. He set goals and stressed Monday night visitation to absentees and newcomers. So successful was the Madison church that churches from across the country flocked to Madison's regular workshops to learn its methods.

North wrote books on church growth and evangelism. He shared his passion for growing churches through numerous programs across the nation: he became editor of the *Gospel Advocate* in 1978; his outreach was extended through the Amazing Grace television program that began in 1971 and extended to 50 stations by the time of his death; some called North "Mr. Enthusiasm," but perhaps "Mr. Outreach" would have been more accurate.

1970-1980
The Soul-Winning Workshops

DISCUSSION QUESTIONS

1. Was your congregation growing during the 1970s? Why or why not?
2. What effect did the workshop movement have on the congregation you attended in the 1970s? Does any event have a similar effect today? Why or why not?
3. Was your congregation influenced in any way by the personality or program ideas of Ira North? How? Does any Christian leader provide this kind of influence on you today?

CHALLENGE QUESTIONS

1. What factors might have contributed to the slowing of growth in the 1970s?
2. Why did such a shift in approaches to evangelism take place?
3. What happened to cause the decline in the number of "big name" preachers?

*Mac Lyon, founder
and host of* In Search
of the Lord's Way

1980-1990

WAVE OF INDIVIDUAL ACTIVISM

"One subject keeps cropping up in sermons, articles, retreats, and lectureships these days - how to interpret the Bible."
-**"THE CHRISTIAN CHRONICLE,"** *September, 1989*

THE 1980s represented new beginnings, times filled both with promise and with a little anxiety. The beginnings came in many areas; one new beginning, in the year 1980, was the inception of Mac Lyon's *Search* television program, which has flourished during a period when other media ministries have waned or dramatically altered their scope or mission. Sponsored and overseen by the Edmond, Oklahoma church, *Search* has grown to be broadcast regularly in 22 states and is seen on satellite systems across North America.

The 1980s also opened with the decision of Oklahoma Christian University to publish *The Christian Chronicle*, which had been established in 1943 by Olan Hicks in Abilene, Texas. Oklahoma Christian's first issue came in September 1981; a *"news* paper, not a *views* paper," the *Chronicle* would, by the late 1980s, reach more than 100,000 homes in all 50 states.

Not long after it began publication, the *Chronicle* told its first "big" story—the $1.5 million drive to take food into Poland, where food shortages had grabbed world attention. The story, the largest such drive in memory, landed on page one.

Then the drives continued, totals grew, and it became routine to raise millions for those suffering from famine or natural disasters. A cadre of leaders expert in such interventions — Don Yelton, Jerry McCaghren, and Kevin McFarland — began to teach us how to serve the needs of an increasingly small planet. These drives became a source of excitement for Christians, a source of visibility for congregations, and a source of help for many in need around the world.

Medical missions and humanitarian projects also soon began to pluck at more than our purse strings. More and more lay Christians began to give up vacation time and energy to provide health-care services in places where medical care was inadequate. Leaders such as Glenn Boyd (Searcy, Arkansas) began coordinating the work of medical professionals who wanted to give their time to provide basic health care, adequate housing, and a Christian message. Partners in Progress began in Little Rock in 1980 to send volunteer healthcare professionals and evangelism teams around the world. By the decade's end, thousands of Christians had volunteered vacation time to go, rather than merely send.

Another grassroots means of spreading the good news, Let's Start Talking, got its start in the 1980s. LST was the brainchild of Oklahoma Christian University English professor Mark Woodward, who was backed by the Dayspring church in Edmond. Training Americans to teach English— and use the Gospels as a text—became the evangelism method of choice at

LET'S START TALKING - www.lst.org - Since 1980, LST has been led by Mark and Sherrylee Woodward and has been training and sending short-term teams of teachers around the world to use English scriptures to teach conversational English—and the spiritual lessons of the gospels—to students interested in learning English.

century's end. Now directed by Woodward and his wife Sherrylee, LST is overseen by the Richland Hills church in Ft. Worth, Texas and continues to send enthusiastic teams around the globe.

The decade also was dominated by publicity regarding legal challenges — first to church discipline issues in Collinsville, Oklahoma (finally solved in late 1989) and later through other lawsuits that seemed to raise leaders' consciousness of our relationships with the culture around us. The lawsuits cast an uneasy pall over much of the decade, in a culture increasingly viewed as antagonistic to faith. When the system of awarding academic credit for Bible classes at Bible chairs and campus ministries was challenged at the University of Texas, a tidal shift in campus ministry models began. It was only one rumble of changing times that campus ministries faced in the 1980s.

"The most visible expression of protest and the most significant effort to revitalize Churches of Christ along specifically sectarian lines occurred in the University of Florida campus ministry led by Charles H. (Chuck) Lucas."

RICHARD T. HUGHES, *Reviving the Ancient Faith*, p. 358.

The Discipling Movement and the ideas of Kip McKean and Al Baird in Boston, Massachusetts also began on campus, growing rapidly both in numbers and influence. It would take most of the 1980s to sort through concerns about the movement and for the mainstream to separate itself.

Mark Woodward, co-founder and director of Let's Start Talking *ministry*

First, however, the "Boston Movement," as it came to be known, would help bring to crisis the threat many church leaders felt about stagnating growth and autonomy issues among churches of Christ. The Movement impressed many with its capacity to attract huge numbers at a time when mainstream churches seemed unable to keep even their own. Accused of being too controlling by publications such as *The Boston Globe*, the movement's leaders made efforts, for most of the decade, to keep open lines of communication and to accommodate mainstream leaders' concerns, before ending most communication with the mainstream by the 1990s.

BOSTON MOVEMENT- A group of churches centered in major cities around the world and led by Charles H. (Chuck) Lucas and protégé Kip McKean. Characterized by radical, moral, and evangelistic zeal, the group maintained a critical-but-communicative stance toward mainstream churches of Christ for most of the 1980s, but by 1990, most ties and connections had been severed.

In the world of ideas, leaders such as Tom Olbricht, Rubel Shelly, Harold Hazelip, and Max Lucado began to speak to broad audiences as they freshened understanding of biblical texts. The addition of a doctoral degree program in Ministry at Abilene Christian University was part of a wave of graduate Bible programs at Christian Universities. Lynn Anderson, then at the Highland church in Abilene, Texas, began to mentor a young generation of ministers. Reuel Lemmons' enthusiasm for world evangelism, stubborn intellectualism, and unorthodox style continued to dominate the *Firm Foundation* and to energize thinking in many camps for most of the decade. But his death at decade's end, as well as the death of Ira North, signaled beginnings of a generational shift among leaders. Indeed, by the end of the decade, one result of this shift involved the increased discussion of hermeneutics among leaders and members.

The 1980s also were a time of explosion in ministries, mostly begun and modeled by large congregations such as Richland Hills (Fort Worth, Texas), which led

Charles H. Lucas (right) helped build "discipling" churches that grew rapidly in the 1980s . By decade's end, few ties remained between these churches and the mainstream.

to specialization in ministries — homeless shelters, AIDS ministries, hospital chaplaincies— frequently led not by paid staff, but often by ordinary members finding renewed energy in serving their communities and one another. As baby boomers began to see the approach of an age-wave, retirement housing and gerontology ministries grew; ACU established a graduate program in gerontology.

"Glasnost" was the watchword at decade's end, as the Berlin Wall that had separated Germany fell and barriers began to shift and erode across the European map. Renewed optimism about world evangelism would be sparked as churches rushed to take advantage of new opportunities. Eastern European Mission, led by John Sudbury, and the World Bible Translation Center, led by Dale Randolph, began to reshape their Cold War methods to adapt to a new era of openness and growth.

LINGUA FRANCA- A language widely used by speakers of many languages as a common currency of communication. At the close of the 20th century, some argued that 80 percent of the world's business, scientific, and academic communication was conducted in English. As a result, millions of school children and adults around the world are busy learning this language as a means of participating in the global economy.

- By R. Scott LaMascus

Tom Olbricht, Pepperdine University theologian and author

Lynn Anderson (circa 1990s) minister of the Highland church, Abilene, Texas

Jack Zorn with a group of young men and boys in New Orleans in 1982 at a "Lads to Leaders" event. Zorn's organization has grown exponentially until today it involves more than 5,000 participants, including young women, in Christian training and service activities each Easter weekend.

1980-1990
Wave of Individual Activism

DISCUSSION QUESTIONS

1. Why were grassroots opportunities so appealing to Christians in the 1980s?
2. Did you, your congregation, or your parents send donations to relief efforts for Poland? Ethiopia? Find someone who did and ask them what they remember.
3. How could your congregation participate in Let's Start Talking in your community?

CHALLENGE QUESTIONS

1. In what way does English as a *lingua franca* compare or contrast to the period of the Pax Romana? Aramaic or Latin as *lingua franca*? Why would the presence of a *lingua franca* be hospitable to the spread of the gospel?
2. What are the biblical bases for a ministry to feed, house, or give medicine to unbelievers? Discuss how this approach differs from other practices, eras, or ideologies.
3. How do you respond to new ideas? How can Christians and congregations respond to change, both positive and negative?

Rubel Shelly, minister at Woodmont Hills church in Nashville, Tennessee

1990-2000

CHANGE AND GROWING DIVERSITY

"...the change taking place among Churches of Christ was no mere reform.... Rather, it was fundamentally a paradigm shift... to an emphasis on the subjective dimensions of the Christian religion —faith, hope and love realized in the lives of believers through the power and grace of God."
-RICHARD T. HUGHES, *from* Reviving the Ancient Faith *(1996)*

THE most skewed history is recent history. Personal involvement, limited perspectives, regional interests, and ecclesiological politics color our perceptions, views that are corrected with more distant and dispassionate assessment. It is difficult, therefore, to appreciate or understand the 1990s until some time has passed. Nevertheless, there are several noteworthy features and trends that will undoubtedly impact the 21st Century.

Mac Lyon and Rubel Shelly represent a diverse fellowship among churches of Christ in the 1990s. Lyon's television program grew from 22 stations in 1990 to 85 in 2000, when he added additional satellite and broadcasting networks. Shelly's influence[1] grew through his consistent appearance at the Pepperdine and Jubilee lectures as well as through his popular writings —including *The Second Incarnation* with Randy Harris — and his website.

---

[1] Web Resource: http://www.faithmatters.com is Rubel Shelly's website containing sermons, essays, bulletin articles, and a discussion forum.

Max Lucado, former missionary to Brazil and minister of the Oak Hills church in San Antonio, Texas, is one of the most-read authors in the contemporary religious world

"Conscientious, Bible-believing Christians throughout the churches of Christ are beginning to ask hard questions about our traditional approach to worship and study." F. LaGard Smith (pictured left), The Cultural Church (1992), p. 13

Three other individuals significantly shaped churches of Christ in the 1990s. Max Lucado, through his many books—*Eye of the Storm* was the first publication by a member of the church of Christ to reach number one on the Evangelical Christian Publishing Association bestseller list—began to nourish a devotional and spiritual hunger awakened within our fellowship.

EVANGELICAL - The conservative Christian world that values the authority of the Bible and a personal ("born-again") relationship with God.

Promise Keepers and the resultant "Men's Movement" among us fed this renewal as well. But Lucado also raised the question of our relationship to the evangelical world, reintroducing churches of Christ to their evangelical neighbors and became a symbol, for good or ill, of a growing alliance with evangelicalism.

Lynn Anderson led a worship and leadership renewal within our fellowship. Anderson's *Navigating the Winds of Change* (1994) introduced us to change in churches of Christ. His "Church that Connects" seminars led in both worship renewal as well as "worship wars," and his *They Smell Like Sheep* (1997) reoriented leadership styles among our elders. The church continues to struggle with both of these renewal movements.

GENERATIONAL SHIFT - The presence of multiple levels of generations within congregations that reflect different values, leadership/worship styles, and needs - thus creating tension in many congregations.

F. LaGard Smith, known for his conservative stance on social issues, rode a rising popularity by addressing concerns that will significantly affect the church in the 21st Century. Writing and lecturing on baptism, gender roles, fellowship, and hermeneutics in the 1990s, he influenced significant elements of our fellowship with his moderate-to-traditional stances. A popular speaker, Smith stood against the rising tide of postmodernism within churches of Christ.

In addition to these thought leaders, the 1990s saw a renewed interest in the historical roots of the American Restoration Movement. Three major interpretations of churches of Christ were published in the 1990s, by Robert Hooper, Richard Hughes, and David Edwin Harrell, along with other, more specific studies by Doug Foster, Tom Olbricht, Michael Casey, and Leonard Allen. This increased awareness generated pursuit of dialogue with other branches of the Stone-Campbell Movement through unity forums, cooperative works, and speaker exchanges.

Yet, throughout this diversity and controversy, the ministry of churches of Christ grew. Most significantly, the fall of the Berlin Wall in 1989 opened Eastern Europe to a flood of church plantings, educational partnerships—such as ones with Russian universities—and short-term missions. The answered prayer of freedom in Eastern Europe galvanized a missionary impulse that also bore fruit in South and Central America, Asia, and especially Africa.

"In 1992, (Rubel) Shelly, Phillip Morrison, and Mike Cope ... launched a new journal called *Wineskins* devoted to communicating the gospel in the language of contemporary culture. Shelly, Morrison, and Cope championed many of the ideals held by Barton Stone, David Lipscomb, and R. H. Boll, but they pointedly backed away from the highly rational orthodoxy that had descended from the Campbell side of the movement."
RICHARD T. HUGHES, *Reviving the Ancient Faith*, p. 372

Exponential growth[2] resulted and, by the end of the decade, church membership in India and Africa each surpassed 700,000 members. Consistent with this renewed missional perspective, the "One Nation Under God" campaign (1991-94) mailed an evangelistic tract to millions of North Americans and Europeans. Ministry also expressed itself in disaster relief efforts for Hurricanes Andrew, Georges, Fran, and

---

[2] Web Resource: http://www.church-of-christ.org is a growing database of churches of Christ throughout the world.

Mike Cope speaking at
the 1993 Pepperdine
University Bible Lectures

Change and Growing Diversity   123

Mitch, tornadoes, the Oklahoma City bombing, and floods—as well as in aid for Croatia, Eastern Europe, and Kosovo.

Ministry also expanded into our inner cities. The Urban Ministry Conference and multiple, inner-city church plants in Houston, Memphis, Atlanta, Nashville, and Birmingham renewed our commitment to the city. These efforts reminded the church of both social and racial barriers to the Gospel as practiced by many suburban congregations.

The 1990s also saw an explosion of influence by our lectureships. Pepperdine's lectures in the West, as well as Jubilee in the East, attracted large crowds and led the church towards renewal. Freed-Hardeman's lectureship experienced renewed success. Significantly, these events reflected a shift away from journal editors as the center of influence. Respected preachers and lectureship speakers gained influence.

POSTMODERNISM -
The current cultural movement that rejects modernist assumptions about indubitable knowledge and is more open to communal narrative experience as faith.

The centers of influence in churches of Christ are now the lectureships, large churches, popular preachers, and schools — probably in that order. Editors, unlike the past, are no longer our "Bishops," as once had been said. The Internet, which promises great influence for the 21st century, was only beginning to grow in the 1990s.

The 1990s displayed tremendous diversity. It was a decade of discussion and change, a shift in churches of Christ from modernism to postmodernism. The church is experiencing a major generational shift: the G.I. generation began to pass away; the Baby Boomers moved into leadership roles; and the Gen Xers voiced their needs. That mixture was sometimes refreshing, sometimes divisive and devastating.

Some believe the future of churches of Christ includes a split along the lines of the one that began the century, in 1906. However, we believe and pray for a "broad middle," one that finds unity in Christ, a unity rooted in the Gospel—the person and work of Christ, the Gospel meaning of baptism and the Lord's Supper, and our hope in the resurrection.

Diversity is here to stay, but unity is too, if we can stand together in Jesus Christ.

- By John Mark Hicks

The Pepperdine University Bible Lectures, directed by Jerry Rushford, brings together speakers and thousands of church members representing a broad spectrum of thought in churches of Christ

1990-2000
Change and Growing Diveristy

DISCUSSION QUESTIONS

1. What person and/or event, having a broad regional or national influence, was most significant in your own spiritual development during the 1990s?
2. Share your own personal experience and perspectives regarding the extent of diversity (both in theological views and ministry) within churches of Christ.
3. What do you think is the most significant ministry development of the 1990s for churches of Christ?

CHALLENGE QUESTIONS

1. As churches of Christ grow increasingly diverse in worship style, ministry, and perspective, is unity a realistic hope? What does a "broad middle" look like?
2. Discuss the author's suggestion that Christology is the ground of unity and provides a hope for the future of churches of Christ. How might our understanding of Christ unite our diversity while respecting the value of diversity?

TEACHING GUIDE
for
"DECADES OF DESTINY"

FOR 12-session BIBLE CLASS QUARTER

I. QUARTER OVERVIEW:

Lesson 1
Introduction to the course, the book, and study of the editors' Introduction

Lesson 2
Study Chapter 1: 19th-Century Origins of Churches of Christ

Lessons 3-12
Study of Chapters 2-12: The Decades of the 20th century, beginning with 1900-1910

II. BASIC LESSON PLAN – 50-minute class

Use this plan for Lessons 3-12 (from 1900-1910 to 1990-2000). Adapt as needed for Lesson 2 on 19th-Century Origins.

1.   5 min.: CHAPTER INTRODUCTION
Ask the class to examine the large photo at the beginning of the chapter (if possible, project the photo) and ask:
a.   What is this photo?
b.   Do you know how it relates to what happened in this decade?
c.   Do you think it represents a key theme for this decade? If so, what or how?

Ideally, students will read each chapter before the class period, but even if not, most likely some will be familiar with the photo after reading its caption and be able to explain its importance. If the photo strikes no chords with students, ask them to keep it in mind while the chapter is read.

2.   15 min.: READING of CHAPTER
To set the stage for the reading, read the quotations or terms that represent highlighted items for the main essay.

Ask class members to read the essay on the decade, and in the chapters where included, the essays on the person of the decade and the event of the decade.

The chapters on the 1980s and the 1990s did not include a person or event because these decades are so recent that making such a selection was difficult or perhaps even meaningless.

3.   10 min.: GENERALIZED DISCUSSION
If examining the photo at the beginning of the chapter did not elicit much response, ask questions a,b,c given above.

And/Or: Ask class members for their reflections or memories about this decade and its people.

Limit discussion as needed to allow for the questions at the end of the chapter.

4.	20 min.: QUESTIONS
	Ask and discuss the "Basic Questions" at the end of the chapter.

	If time, and if appropriate, ask and discuss the "Challenge
	Questions."

If the class finds that the discussion and reminiscences could last much longer than one class period, consider expanding the study to two quarters. For the decades where appropriate, read and discuss the essay during the first class period, the person and event during the second class period.

Appendix A

NOMINEES

for *The Christian Chronicle's* Person and Event

for Each Decade of the 20th Century

The nominators' names and rationales have been eliminated from this listing. A listing including that information can be found at www.christianchronicle.org. See Archives.

1900-1910
NOMINEES FOR EVENT OF THE DECADE:
1906 census
R. H. Boll becomes front page editor of the *Gospel Advocate*, 1909
Childers Classical Institute (now Abilene Christian University) and Freed-Hardeman College founded
Establishment of Potter Bible College, 1901
Harding-White debate over special providence, 1910
Russell-White debate between L. S. White and Charles Taze Russell, founder of the Jehovah's Witnesses, 1908
G. H. P. Showalter named editor of the *Firm Foundation*, 1908

1900 - 1910
NOMINEES FOR PERSON OF THE DECADE:
G. P. Bowser
James A. Harding
David Lipscomb
W. W. Otey

1910 - 1920
NOMINEES FOR EVENT OF THE DECADE:
Closing of Cordell Christian College
Death of David Lipscomb, Nov. 11, 1917
Removal of R. H. Boll as front-page editor of the *Gospel Advocate* (start of premillennial controversy), 1915
Reversal of *Gospel Advocate* editorial position away from pacifism, 1917
Jesse Sewell becomes president of Abilene Christian College, 1912

1910 - 1920
NOMINEES FOR PERSON OF THE DECADE:
J. N. Armstrong
R. H. Boll
T. B. Larimore
David Lipscomb
G. H. P. Showalter

1920 - 1930
NOMINEES FOR EVENT OF THE DECADE:
S. H. Hall's move to the Sichel Street church, Los Angeles
N. B. Hardeman's Tabernacle Meetings, Nashville, Tenn.

1920 - 1930
NOMINEES FOR PERSON OF THE DECADE:
Sarah Andrews

H. Leo Boles
A. L. Cassius
S. H. Hall
Marshall Keeble
Jesse P. Sewell
G.H. P. Showalter
Foy E. Wallace

1930 - 1940
NOMINEES FOR EVENT OF THE DECADE:
George Benson named Harding College president
Christian Leader established, 1939
Urbanization of the church

1930 - 1940
NOMINEES FOR PERSON OF THE DECADE:
H. Leo Boles
G. C. Brewer
Clinton Davidson
George W. DeHoff
N. B. Hardeman
George Pepperdine
Foy E. Wallace, Jr.

1940-50
NOMINEES FOR EVENT OF THE DECADE:
Sponsorship of European missions by the Broadway church, Lubbock
World War II-era missions

1940-50
NOMINEES FOR PERSON OF THE DECADE:
George Benson
G. C. Brewer
The ex-G.I.s
Otis Gatewood
Olan Hicks
Marshall Keeble

Andy T. Ritchie

1950 - 1960
NOMINEES FOR EVENT OF THE DECADE:
Cogdill-Woods Debates
Herald of Truth begun
Issue of Church Cooperation
Lubbock Christian College begun, 1957

1950 - 1960
NOMINEES FOR PERSON OF THE DECADE:
G. P. Bowser
Otis Gatewood
B. C. Goodpasture
V. E. Howard
Marshall Keeble
Jack Lewis
Lemoine Lewis
F. W. Mattox
James Walter Nichols
E. Lucien Palmer
W. B. West

Guy N. Woods
M. Norvel and Helen M. Young

1960 - 1970
NOMINEES FOR EVENT OF THE DECADE:
Building of Manhattan (New York) church
The Church of Christ exhibit at the New York World's Fair
Pioneer years of Christian education in the Northern United States
Carl Spain's ACU speech on integrating schools

1960 - 1970
NOMINEES FOR PERSON OF THE DECADE:
Jimmy Allen
J. C. Bailey
Batsell Barrett Baxter
Marshall Keeble
Carl Ketcherside
Reuel Lemmons
Juan Monroy
K. C. Moser
Ira North
Carl Spain
"Big Don" Williams

<u>1970 - 1980</u>
NOMINEES FOR EVENT OF THE DECADE:

Growth of secondary and primary Christian
  schools
Growth of World Bible School
The Herald of Truth meeting of "liberal" and
  "conservative" leaders in Memphis
Tulsa International Soul Winning Workshop
  begun

<u>1970 - 1980</u>
NOMINEES FOR PERSON OF THE DECADE:

J. C. Bailey
Batsell Barrett Baxter
Alan Bryan
Clifton L. Ganus, Jr.
Don Gardner
Berkeley Hackett
Jimmy Lovell
Chuck Lucas
Ira North
Marvin Phillips
Ira Rice
Landon Saunders
Guy N. Woods
Norvel Young

<u>1980 - 1990</u>
NOMINEES FOR EVENT OF THE DECADE:

Expansion of "Search" with Mac Lyon
Rubel Shelly's Centerville Speech and his
  publication of *"I Just Want to Be a Christian"*

<u>1980 - 1990</u>
NOMINEES FOR PERSON OF THE DECADE:

Lynn Anderson
Leroy Garrett
Otis Gatewood
Harold Hazelip
Ira North
Tom Olbricht
Rubel Shelly
Stanley Shipp

<u>1990 - 2000</u>
NOMINEES FOR EVENT OF THE DECADE:

Church planting in Central and Eastern
  Europe
Jubilee
Pepperdine Bible Lectures
Tulsa Workshop

<u>1990 - 2000</u>
NOMINEES FOR PERSON OF THE DECADE:

Lynn Anderson
Max Lucado
Mac Lyon
Jerry Rushford
Rubel Shelly
Helen Young

Appendix B

SELECT BIBLIOGRAPHY

Allen, C. Leonard, Richard T. Hughes, and Michael R. Weed. *The Worldly Church: A Call for Biblical Renewal.* Abilene: ACU Press, 1988.

Allen, C. Leonard and Richard T. Hughes. *Discovering Our Roots: The Ancestry of Churches of Christ.* Abilene: ACU Press, 1988.

Bradshaw, Thomas G. *R. H. Boll: Controversy and Accomplishment Among Churches of Christ.* Louisville, KY: Word and Work, 1998.

Brewer, Grover Cleveland. *Forty Years on the Firing Line.* Kansas City, MO: Old Paths, 1948.

---. *A Story of Toil and Tears of Love and Laughter: Being the Autobiography of G. C. Brewer, 1884-1956.* Murfreesboro, TN: DeHoff Publications, 1957.

Casey, Michael W. *Saddlebags, City Streets and Cyberspace.* Abilene: ACU Press, 1995.

Childers, Jeff W., Douglas A. Foster, and Jack R. Reese. *The Crux of the Matter: Crisis, Tradition, and the Future of the Churches of Christ.* Abilene: ACU Press, 2000.

Doran, Adron and J. E. Choate. *The Christian Scholar: A Biography of Hall Laurie Calhoun.* Nashville: Gospel Advocate, 1985.

Dunnavant, Anthony L., Richard T. Hughes, and Paul M. Blowers. *Founding Vocation and Future Vision: The Self-Understanding of the Disciples of Christ and the Churches of Christ.* St. Louis: Chalice, 2001.

Foster, Douglas A. *Will the Cycle Be Unbroken? Churches of Christ Face the 21st Century.* Abilene: ACU Press, 1994.

Garrett, Leroy. *The Stone-Campbell Movement.* Joplin, MO: College Press, 1994.

Harrell, David Edwin. *The Churches of Christ in the 20th Century: Homer Hailey's Journey of Faith.* Tuscaloosa: University of Alabama Press, 2000.

Hicks, John Mark. "Alexander Campbell on Christians Among the Sects," *Baptism and the Remission of Sins.* David W. Fletcher, ed. Joplin, MO: College, 1990: 171-202.

Holloway, Gary and Douglas A. Foster. *Renewing God's People: A Concise History of Churches of Christ.* Abilene: ACU Press, 2001.

Hooper, Robert E. *A Distinct People: A History of Churches of Christ in the 20th Century.* West

Monroe, LA: Howard Publishing Co., 1993.

Hughes, Richard T., Nathan O. Hatch, and David Edwin Harrell. *American Origins of Churches of Christ.* Douglas A. Foster, ed. Abilene: ACU Press, 1999.

Hughes, Richard T. and R. Roberts. *The Churches of Christ.* Westport, CT: Greenwood Press, 2001.

Hughes, Richard T. *Reviving the Ancient Faith: The Story of Churches of Christ in America.* Grand Rapids: Eerdmans, 1996.

Long, Loretta M. *The Life of Selina Campbell: A Fellow Soldier in the Cause of Restoration.* Tuscaloosa: University of Alabama Press, 2001.

Lynn, Mac. *Churches of Christ in the United States, 2000.* Nashville: 21st Century, 2000.

Olbricht, Thomas H. *Hearing God's Voice: My Life with Scripture in Churches of Christ.* Abilene: ACU Press, 1996.

Patterson, Noble and Terry J. Gardner, eds. *Foy E. Wallace: Soldier of the Cross.* Fort Worth: Wallace Memorial Fund, 1999.

Richardson, Robert. *Communings in the Sanctuary.* Orange, CA: New Leaf, 2000.

Sears, L. C. *The Eyes of Jehovah: The Life and Faith of James Alexander Harding.* Nashville: Gospel Advocate, 1970.

---. *For Freedom: The Biography of John Nelson Armstrong.* Austin, TX: Sweet Publishing, 1969.

Shelly, Rubel and Randall J. Harris. *The Second Incarnation: A Theology for the 21st Century Church.* Abilene: HillCrest Publishing, 2001.

West, Earl Irvin. *The Search for the Ancient Order,* Vols. 1–4. Germantown, TN: Religious Book Service, 1950-1987.

Woodroof, James S. *The Church in Transition.* Searcy, AR: Bible House, 1990.

Selected Web Sites

McMillan, Jim. www.Bible.ACU.Edu/Stone-Campbell/ This comprehensive site contains electronic texts, links on Restoration Movement history, and additional materials.

Rollman, Hans. http://www.mun.ca/rels/restmov/index.html This comprehensive site contains electronic texts, links on Restoration Movement history, and additional materials. It can also be accessed through the Abilene Christian University website under Ministry Resources (Stone-Campbell).

NOTES